CLOUD COVER

CLOUD COVER

By
Andrea Rogers

Publisher:

neue cadence

Cloud Cover
©2025 Andrea Rogers

All rights reserved. No part of this book may be reproduced in any form of by any electric or mechanical means including information storage and retrieval systems—except in the case of brief quotations embodied in critical articles or reviews—without permission in writing from its author.

Published by neue cadence
Andrea Rogers
Tempe, AZ
akrogersart@gmail.com

ISBN-13: 978-0-9963613-5-4

Library of Congress Control Number: 2025906438

Cover design: RBAndersonart@gmail.com

Book Shepherd Ann Narcisian Videan, ANVidean.com

DEDICATION

For my Listener, David Rosen.

TABLE OF CONTENTS

Chapter 1
The deepest wounds show no blood.

1.	The Beginning	1
2.	The Cavern	4
3.	Fifty Years from Now	6
4.	The Night of the Angels, Part One	9
5.	The Night of the Angels, Part Two	12
6.	The Man with the Red Cape	16
7.	Happy Birthday, Jesus	17
8.	Freed	19

Chapter 2
Invisible evidence.

9.	Literal Discipline	21
10.	Family History	26
11.	After She'd Seen Honolulu	29
12.	Monster-in-Law	32

Chapter 3
We are forever children.

13.	Anointed	34
14.	Escape	37
15.	It Was the Uniform	39
16.	A Very Short Ride	42
17.	The Horrible Woman Next Door	44
18.	The White House	47
19.	The Fanner 50	52
20.	Follow Your Nose	55
21.	The Puzzle	59
22.	The Hand in the Casket	62
23.	Thanksgiving	64
24.	Double Bubble Trouble	70

Chapter 4
We find our own way, no matter what.

25. A Very Long Ride	72
26. Lost in Arizona	78
27. One Divided into Two Equals Trouble	81
28. Remedial Math	85
29. From Books to Bombs to Baseball	87
30. Pure and Shiny, for Now	92
31. Privileges	96
32. Becoming a Girl	100
33. The Incident at the Silver Pool	103
34. Fluteless	104
35. Paleontology or Biology	107
36. Burial Rights	110
37. Public Speaking	112
38. Cooking Class	116
39. Analyze This	118
40. Raising the Dead	121
41. A Snake at the Door	123
42. Cat Tales	127
43. Promises and Premonitions	130
44. November 22, 1963	134
45. The Rat Study	137
46. My Messenger	141

Chapter 5
It had to be me. There was no one else.

47. The Terrorist and the Politician	144
48. Locked Out	148
49. Stinkin' Sweet Revenge	152
50. Way Too Young	156

Chapter 6

> Everybody, soon or late,
> sits down to a banquet of consequences.
> —Robert Louis Stevenson

51. The Attic Dream	159
52. Art Production Plus	165
53. He Knows!	170
54. Sparks Will Fly	172
55. Face Off	175
56. Crown of Thorns	179
57. Recovery	183

Chapter 7

When you make your own world, you best hold on to not fall.

58. The Warning, Guidance, and The Rescue	186
59. Silver into Gold	190
60. Looking for America	194
61. Drawing Lessons	198
62. Group	201
63. The Doll, the Flag, and Sweet Potato Pie	204
64. Wagon Wheels and Seashells	207

Chapter 8

> Students can't drive you crazy unless you give them the keys.
> —Joe Martin, aka TheEducatorMotivator.com

65. Contemporary Temporary	210
66. Rural Lives	216
67. My Criminals	221
68. Joining the Circus	229
69. Play Their Games	233
70. War Torn	238

Chapter 9
When everything changes, grow up.

71. I Declare	246
73. Fifty Plus Four	251

Epilogue   256

Discussion Questions for Book Clubs

Acknowledgments

About the Author

PROLOGUE

Before we had a sense of our own power, the powers around us molded us. Before we had self-awareness, before we developed memory, things happened to us. Unprotected and innocent, attitudes, words and events formed human beings. These hidden influences became our character and our understanding of the world.

Some of us escaped.

To the reader: Keep reading past the dreadful beginning stories to discover the childlike humor, the challenges of mother/child relationships, the questions about race and religion, and how to be a girl. The rest of the stories reveal responses to a secret stored for fifty years.

– Chapter 1 –

I. THE BEGINNING

I knelt before the light. Unborn and waiting. A question would be asked of me, the question all were asked. At once I heard and felt a mighty wind, a wind that would carry me forever, powerful, within and around the space where I was to be formed. Within this wind I heard a gentle voice.

Why do you desire life? What birthright do you seek?

I knew what I wanted. "Bravery," I replied.

Warmth and kindness surrounded me.

"That you will have," the Voice continued in a slow and steady rhythm, "but only after torment. Torment will either force you to be brave or it will destroy you."

A pause.

The light strengthened. "However, with bravery comes loneliness and despair. They are joined together, locked in place. These cannot be avoided if you seek to be brave." I wondered if I could ask for more.

And then.

"What more do you want for your life?"

I knew what I wanted.

"To be true," I replied. "to myself and all I meet. True in all I do and say, never deceitful or seeking harm to another."

I waited.

The Voice in the wind whispered sadly. "This cannot be granted. It is beyond any human ability, as all are certain to lie, but because you asked, you will be among the first of the true, imperfect but sincere. You will undoubtedly recognize your fall from this quality each day as you hold a regret or attain your goal."

"One more," the Voice pulsed louder as the light increased.

"I want to be free," I pleaded, "Free to be myself, not owned, not pushed."

"This you may earn, as all are enslaved in life. I grant you freedom, but it will come only after you suffer its cost. Freedom is not understood, or appreciated except after bearing the burden of enslavement."

A moment more and then I heard.

"What is done cannot be undone. Life and longing you now face."

The light became a wavering mirror and within it I saw my own reflection. The bravery, the truth, the freedom; the life I would live had become a crown of thorns. Yet, as I felt my soul lifted, as I began to float away, the stems in my headdress turned green and flowering buds shot forth, tangled in their abundance and wonderful in color, and as I rose I saw all humanity, adorned with the same crown of grief, joined in a common destiny, wearing also, the blossoms of the possibilities in life.

2. THE CAVERN

The slapping sound of water against the boat awakens me, yet I am in a dream unlike any other. My spirit is observing another reality yet aware that I am asleep in life.

Seated behind a hooded figure, I feel no fear. I am secure. It is not me death is looking for.

The channel we move through is dark and narrow, the water black. Our small boat rocks from side to side, as if being rowed, but there are no oars. We simply move, gliding slowly toward an open arch where sunlight is streaming in from outside.

We enter a caldera, the center of what was once a volcano now filled with water. The sun beams down from just above the walls and I can tell the time is late afternoon. Our craft veers to the right tracing the walls where multiple small caves stand carved from the rock. At the entrance of each cave a fire burns, illuminating the water, as the sun disappears, falling behind the wall.

Now the firelight guides our journey. We move closer to the caves. Hugging the walls, I look into each one. I catch only a glimpse of a figure behind each fire.

At the entrance of one of the caves the boat balances momentarily. I am close enough to feel the heat. I hear the crackling of the fire. Who is this behind the flames?

I recognize him. It is my father.

This must be Hell.

3. FIFTY YEARS FROM NOW

> When the woodworm burns
> And the stars are still
> creeping over the hill,
> The little children say their prayers.

Stunned into wakefulness, sunlight streaming into my room, I forced my eyes open. I began looking, looking for evidence. My hands felt for wounds. I checked my stomach and legs. Blood, there should be blood. On the floor. Was there any there? The sheets should have blood. I got up and moved the bedding. Nothing. The light hurt my eyes. I was shaking. I traced the path to the front door. The screen was open. No footprints. No drops of blood. The bear that had eaten me last night got away. I ached in my stomach. I felt I would disappear.

I had felt his mouth, his hot breathing, and his drooling, but in my sleep, I could not fight him. I could not wake up. It was real. I knew it, but where was the proof? Without proof, who would believe me?

I had heard my mother talking on the phone just yesterday, "Four-year olds have such imaginations," she laughed.

What would she say if I told her a bear had been in my room last night?

Who would believe me? I was shaking, losing me. Who could I trust? My legs were crumbling. I had no one, but myself. I could trust only myself.

I realized that years would pass, and I would lose this memory that has destroyed me. It would have to be saved somehow.

A camera. My father's camera was in the closet. I knew where they kept it.

I stood in the kitchen door waiting for my mother to notice me. "Get the camera," I demanded. She looked at me. "I need my raincoat and umbrella too. I want you to take my picture.

"Why do you need your raincoat? It isn't raining."

"I know, but you can't take a picture in the rain. I need my umbrella too. Get it and the camera." She reached up into the closet, handed me the camera, and pulled out my red raincoat and my clear plastic umbrella.

"Now what?"

"Take my picture." I handed her the camera. I needed evidence of this day to save myself, and this is how I would get it. On film, forever. A document to capture what I needed to remember.

In the yard, I put on my raincoat and tightened the belt securely. Hands shaking, I opened my umbrella. I gripped it tightly with both hands, staring into the lens. I made my body into a solid thing.

"Get closer!" I had to make sure I would someday recognize an image of what would be the past, being sent into the future. "Get closer," I called to my mother.

She took two baby steps.

"Closer!"

The camera would take it away. It would hold me here, safe, stored away. "I willed it into my mind. I *will* remember in fifty years," I thought. "That way they will both be dead." I calculated my parent's ages. My mother was 40 and my dad 39. "They will be dead when I remember this day."

Past my elementary school years...past girl scouts...past high school...and into my adult married life. Then I would remember. Then I could be safe.

Snap! It was done.

4. THE NIGHT OF THE ANGELS
PART ONE

Not real, is how the dream appeared. More like a repeated image and a sensation was how it came to me. It wasn't a dream; it was physical to me. I felt weighed down, and I couldn't move my arms or legs. In my mind I saw a cloud above me and with it came its heaviness, always with the feeling that something was on top of me.

Each morning, I had forgotten about it and went through the day as always, but again it would come and when it did, I tried to remember, while still sleeping, to examine it, to understand what was happening. It repeated and repeated, not every night, but often enough to become a memory attached to sleep. I decided to find out what was causing this experience.

I imagined myself swimming. I would swim upward as fast and as hard as I could and swim out of my sleep. I would come awake enough to look, to see what was doing this to me.

It was winter when I found myself once again under this cloud, holding me down, but this time I knew what to do. I felt as if I were under water, deep within an ocean, but I knew I could swim to wakefulness this time and I did. The very second I reached the shore I kicked back. I kicked out from under the cloud. I dug my heels into the sand, being my own bed, and shoved my body backward against the wall. My eyes were hard to open, and I struggled to see. Pulling my knees to my chest, I squinted into the darkened room.

I saw a head, the head of a man. The head of a man who I gradually recognized as my father. I lost my vision and I lost my sense of who I was. I began to shake. I looked through him and saw nothing. I was suddenly blind, staring, but unseeing, but now I knew.

Time stopped. I shook uncontrollably, shivering unbearably. I had no sense of time. I was frozen.

At some point in the timelessness, I heard his feet as he padded from the room, the bear I had met before. I had not moved, nor could I. I no longer had a father. I did not have a home. I understood how terribly my life had changed. The person responsible for me, wasn't. I had no safe place any longer. This could not be my home. So, I left.

Eventually, at some point in my emptiness, as what may have been hours passed over me, I heard laughter, light, floating laughter, like that of babies, joyful, like tinkling bells. I went to the window and looked out but saw nothing. They were still laughing, and it sounded close, so I put on my robe and slippers, opened the window and climbed out.

The snow crunched under my feet, and I could see the two of them ahead of me, lingering mid-air, playing pattycake. They were both naked and I wondered if they were boys or girls. I quietly moved closer to look. I had no trouble seeing them as the night was as bright as day. The snow gleamed and the whole yard was illumined but the source was not apparent.

I stood below them just near enough to see them both clearly. and having been unable to see the sex of either, I decided to ask a question, "Can I play too?"

My presence must have alarmed them because the one closest to me looked the way a kid does when he or she is caught doing something wrong. At that, they vanished. Just like that, they were gone. The world darkened, the light, too, vanished and I was very, very cold.

5. THE NIGHT OF THE ANGELS
PART TWO

The cold awakened me to the real world where I now stood alone. The angels had disappeared. Thinking that I should try to get back inside the house, I looked around for rocks to throw at my parents' window hoping to wake them, but the snow covered the ground evenly, no bare ground anywhere. I pushed snow aside with my fingers and felt they would freeze so I gave up that idea.

I wondered if the screen door on the front porch was left unlocked, so I tried it, but it was locked and now my fingers were really cold. I tucked my hands into the sleeves of my corduroy robe and my fingers felt warmer against my arms. I sat on the steps and leaned against the screen door. My thoughts warmed under the glow of the streetlight on the corner of our lot.

Remembering the angels, I pulled my knees up to my chest and still shivering, waited for morning. I had heard that dying by freezing was painless, like going to sleep. I was certain I would die, so when I awakened the following morning with a sheet above my head, I believed that I was in heaven under the wing of an angel, but I had not died. My mother had merely fixed a sheet over me with a vaporizer running to help my raspy breath.

Disappointed that I wouldn't be with the angels, I went back to sleep and forgot everything about the night before. I had also forgotten how to talk.

Silence

Time disappeared. I have no recall of the events in the house. I stopped talking, not on purpose. I just wasn't there.

Where was I?

Where did I go?

I have no recall of this time in my life, nor do I know how long it lasted, but finally I came back.

It was my mother, holding my hand, climbing stairs together, going into a big stone building, and releasing me into the care of a woman wearing a white jacket. She took me into a large room and pointed to the shelves of toys, more than I could imagine.

"You may play with anything you like." Her voice was kind.

From across the room, I saw a dollhouse, then I looked back at her.

"Would you like the dollhouse?

I nodded.

"And a family?"

"Just a little girl and her mother," I whispered.

With the dollhouse on the table in front of me, I held the two small dolls. Together they climbed the stairs. At the top, just as the dolls turned as if to go down, without warning the child pushed the mother down the stairs, killing her.

I felt a sudden flood of relief as she tumbled downward.

The woman spoke, "Do you have bad dreams?"

"No. They aren't dreams."

"What is it then?"

I looked at here intently. *Would she believe me?*

"There's a bear. It's real!"

"Does it chase you?"

I shook my head. "No. It eats me."

There was a long pause and the session was over.

She stood up, took my hand with a gentle squeeze and I was returned to my mother, who pulled me toward her as we prepared to leave.

"She will need to come back." The woman spoke with authority, keeping her gaze on us as my mother gripped my hand. She put her arms across her chest and said, "Bring her back. We are not through."

Ignoring the woman's words, my mother kept me close as I tried to look back over my shoulder. But I saw her one last time, my savior standing at the top of the stairs in front of clear glass cubes of light, shining like an angel who I knew would disappear.

6. THE MAN WITH THE RED CAPE

The only other memory I have of my time of silence is a visit to an art museum. How long we had been there or what paintings we had passed in the numerous hallways I do not know. I was not looking. I was listening. All reality, at this point, consisted of sound. Only sounds. I heard the echoes of footsteps, overlapping feet in long passageways, some close, some fading away, people passing us, unseen.

When I did look up, I was standing in front of a man with a red cape casually thrown over his shoulder. As I stood there seeing art for the very first time, he said to me, "Be an artist. Then you will never die."

7. HAPPY BIRTHDAY, JESUS

It was the night before Christmas, and we were ready to leave the house to attend church. I had returned to myself, but something had happened to my memory of the night I met the angels.

I had no cause for alarm, since the terror of the discovery regarding my father and the astonishment at seeing angels in my yard were lost memories, I acted as always. Both unbelievable events were glued together like photographs in an album facing each other, exposed to heat and melded into one, protecting my mind. I reached for my father's hand as always, but as my fingers touched his, he pried his hand free, pushing my hand from his. Salt stung my eyes. A sob caught in my throat, but I wouldn't cry. Not me. I had another father, one who loved me, one I could trust. I wouldn't cry because of him. Not me. I didn't need him anymore. I only needed a place to grow up. I would let him do that for me, but that was all.

After church I did what needed to be done. I asked my mother for a Christmas card. I made it into a birthday card instead.

In my best printing in big letters, I wrote-Happy Birthday Jesus. Of course, I could not mail the card, I knew that, but I also knew that He knew and would never hurt me.

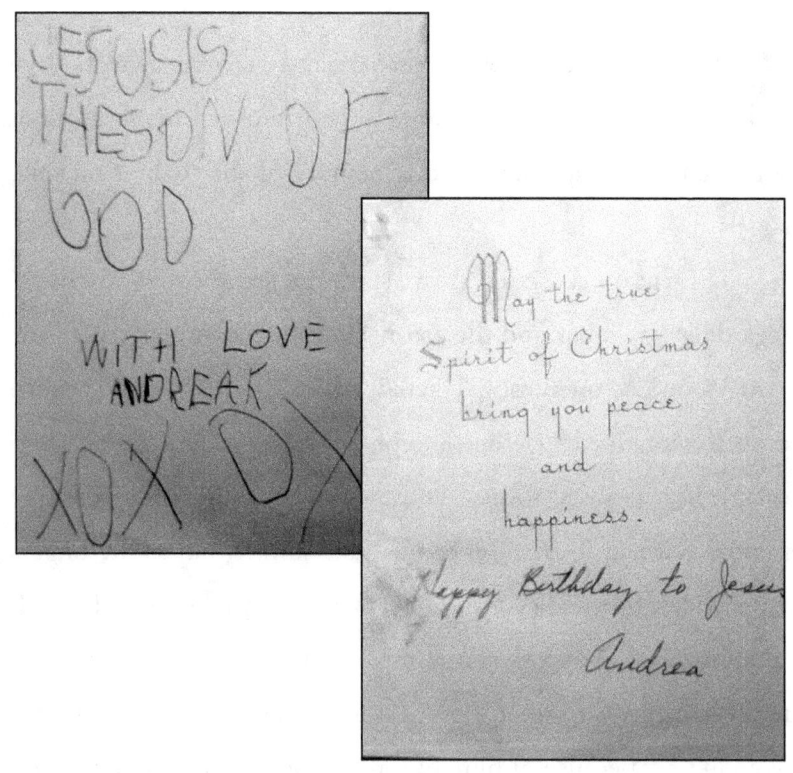

8. FREED

Things changed suddenly. I no longer took baths with my little sister.

"You're a big girl now. You are seven and you can bathe yourself," my mother proclaimed. I was given Cleo, the goldfish from the movie *Pinocchio*, as my new bathing companion. I played with her until she became moldy from water squeezed in and out of her pouty mouth. Baths that used to be fun with my sister, playing mermaids, were now lonely and boring.

There were no more bedtime stories or lullabies sung to me either.

"How do I go to sleep?"

"You'll learn," she said. But some nights, after dozing off, I would wake to hear angry voices.

Finally, my father began working nights and I seldom saw him.

I was treated differently in another way. I was freed. I no longer had to ask to go somewhere or be told when to return. I had the complete run of the neighborhood. Maybe this could be considered neglect, but I relished it. I would leave the house and randomly decide on a direction. A few streets away new houses appeared, piles of wood and carpet samples lay abandoned, remnants of the good fortune of new homeowners. In a vacant lot, I ran up and down hills. Friends showed up, new ones. I read their comic books, sampled their snacks and played with their pets, but most of the time I hung around the backyard. Everyone knew where to find me and I would initiate the regular childhood games, hide and seek or shadow tag, as the day darkened. The only rule was, "Come home when the streetlight turns on."

From then on I made all my own decisions. I learned from this time to take charge of myself. I did not get in trouble, usually. I ran my own life, seldom if ever consulting with my mother.

Any mistakes made were my own.

I asked for nothing.

– Chapter 2 –

9. LITERAL DISCIPLINE

In my childhood I was only spanked once, and I deserved it. The rest of the time, my mother, my only actual parent, used poetry, songs and stories to put me in my place. There were also random shrill outbursts of a phrase I did not understand, but which immediately ended any activity I was doing, resulting in my exiting the house.

She would pull at her hair and screech, "You give me the screaming mimis."

Time to leave. I did not connect my behavior to her anxiety. *What had caused this?* I was only being myself. I did not know what "mimis" were until my adult years when I learned that this was the word for the sound of a rapid firing machine gun from the front lines of World War I.

Bedtime had the musical part. My sister's lullaby went like this:

"Shabobin Shabobin Shalawa
and Jalawa Kookalagoomba.
Shabobin Shabobiin Shalawa
my bambino go to sleep.
All the stars are in the sky ready to say good night.
Can't you see your dolly's sleeping too?
Close your drowsy little eyes. Mother will hold you tight while she sings this lullaby to you."

Repeat... end with...
"My bambino go to sleep."

This was my lullaby:

"'Oh, don't you remember how a long time ago
two poor little babes whose names we don't know
were stolen away on a fine summer's day
and left in the woods,' we've heard people say.
They sobbed and they sighed, and they bitterly cried. Those poor little babes.
They lay down and died.
And when they were dead, the robin so red brought strawberry leaves and over them spread,
and sang them this song the whole night long.
Those poor little babes… Those poor little babes."

Was this supposed to help me go to sleep? I know it opened my imagination.

Who took the children and why were they left alone to die?

I thought the robin was especially sweet and the leaves were comforting. I liked the rhyme and the rhythm. However, why did my mother choose this song for me? That made me wonder. I fell asleep thinking hard about all those questions.

A story she told me may not have been true, but it scared me, connected to a game a neighbor girl started: Palm Reading. She lined us all up, taking turns. I heard her tell one of the kids that his lifeline was short, and he would die young. *Was my lifeline short?* I examined both hands. *Which one has the longest line?* Before I could decide, it was my turn.

"Hmm?" She looked at both of my hands holding first one and then the other, finally deciding on the right one. I held my breath.

"Your lifeline has three cut lines across it," she looked up at me as if I understood the seriousness of this.

"Uh, ok. What does that mean?" *Would I die young?*

"Disaster, three close calls or some things that are really, horrible will happen, but the lines are at the end, near your wrist, so you don't have to worry for a long, long time. Next!"

But I was worried, so I decided I should ask my mom. "I want to go to a palm reader, a real one," I told her.

"That is not a good idea," she said.

"Why," I asked, worried that I would have a lifetime of worrying about my lifeline.

"Well, I have a friend who knew someone who went to palm reader."

"And? What happened?"

"She went to downtown Indianapolis. The place she went to was just a small pink house on a busy street. She went in and sat in a room in front to wait. There was another area behind a thin beaded curtain through which she could see two women sitting at a table. On the center of the table was a crystal ball, but the older woman wasn't using it, she was holding the hand of the younger one. This visitor could hear them talking. The palm reader was talking calmly, but the customer's voice was loud and angry.

"Why won't you read my palm?' she demanded. "I came a long way to do this! I want my money back!"

'You can have your money... here,' she handed her back her cash, not looking at her. 'I'm sorry. I just can't. I can't read your palm.'

"The customer was so distressed she got up in a hurry, ran through the room and out the door right into the street without looking. There was a screech of brakes and a thud. The two women jumped up and ran outside. She was lying under a truck, killed instantly."

My mouth dropped open, "But why wouldn't she read the woman's palm? If she had just read her palm she wouldn't have been killed."

"That's the question, the woman waiting asked also."

"But why?"

"The palm reader finally told her, "Because she faced imminent death."

The story cured me. No fortune telling or palm reading for me. I was done. Was the story true? I don't know. My mother didn't have many friends as I remember and the one's I knew seemed normal, not the kind who knew people who would visit a fortune teller. Still?

Then I learned a new song from the radio, "Que Sera, Sera; What will be, will be." I quit looking at my hands. I would wait and see what fate would bring.

10. FAMILY HISTORY

This town of Oblong, once named Henpeck, has remained small from the beginning. In the 1800's, settlers stopped here only to stock up on their way west. Now there are nearly 1500 citizens living there. Surrounded by corn fields and oil drills, it had no room to grow.

I visited there again in my twenties with my husband and parents. One quiet afternoon when no one was around, my aunt told me she had something to show me. I sat with her as she opened a photo album. She held up a photo of a baby girl.

"Do you know who this is?" It was a black and white photo, but I saw a pale little girl with light blue eyes, so light they seemed nearly white.

"No," I said, "Who is she?"

"This is Lila, your grandmother's daughter."

"There was a daughter? What happened to her?" Never knowing of her existence, I was more than a little curious.

"She was Zenith's first child, born before she married Ora, your grandfather."

My first thought was, "Oh my! How hard that must have been here, in a town so small that no matter where you looked you could see someone in their home through a window, no fences, no privacy. Everyone would know.

But the story got worse. "The baby's father was your grandfather, Zenith's own father."

"What?" I was stunned. "The baby was the result of incest?"

"It happened back then," she explained. "To try to hide the truth, her parents raised the child as their own, making her Zenith's little sister."

I wondered, Why is she telling me this?

There was more to show me, a scrapbook. "Your grandmother kept the details of every event in the newspaper where Lila's name was mentioned, every birthday party she attended, every dance, her graduation."

It seemed so sad, but the story got worse.

"What happened to her? "Where is she now"

My aunt continued, "There was a car accident. She was driving on a country road at the same time a group of picnickers were heading back to town. Somehow there was a collision, and everyone was thrown from their vehicles. One young woman, pregnant at the time, lost her baby."

"And Lila?" I asked.

"She was blamed for the accident, so she left Oblong as soon as she could. No one ever knew where she went."

Of course, *someone had to be blamed*. I couldn't stop thinking about the story.

So very sad, for everyone, everyone except my great grandfather.

"What happened to him," I ask.

"He slit his own throat, but the knife was too dull."

That was enough for me.

Recently, I tried to learn more about Lila. I found her name in the census records living in Jay, Indiana in 1930. That would make her twenty, around the same time the accident happened. That was all I could discover. I so wanted to know more. I hope she had a life. I hope she found love. I hope she was happy.

But why did my aunt tell me this story and what did it have to do with me?

II. AFTER SHE'D SEEN HONOLULU

When I got home from school, I was supposed to come in the kitchen door. The screen door on the porch leading to the living room stayed locked for some reason. On this day of first grade, I was about to open the back door.

"Stop right there. Go around to the front. It's open."

When I came through the house to where my mother was in the kitchen, I was stunned to see her slinging yellow paint on our black floor. I had not heard of Jackson Pollack but maybe she had.

Is she crazy? Does she just want to brighten the room? Is this an improvement?

I didn't know and I couldn't tell.

As time went on and I knew her better, I understood why she had to do it. It wasn't just the blackness of the floor; it was the bleakness of her life.

My parents went to the same high school in a town so small it was one square mile around, surrounded by corn fields, a square town called Oblong, a place so limiting that I knew every crack in the sidewalk after only one afternoon of roller skating.

My mother couldn't wait to get out of there. It was World War II and there was plenty of excitement to be had. Off she went to join the Women's Army Corp., serving in Hawaii. On the island she drove a jeep, smoked cigarettes, dated Marines, picked coconuts, danced the hula and went to nightclubs. I found the photos to prove it.

"Don't tell anyone that I was in the WAC's, she said. They had such a bad reputation."

It was verified in a letter to her mother I found, unsent, describing the night the MPs caught her out past curfew. It was her third date that evening.

She would never have met my father if not for my grandmother getting her hair done back in good old Oblong, Illinois. The beautician was my mother's sister.

I can imagine the conversation:

"My son is in the army."

"Oh, where is he stationed?"

"Hawaii."

"So is my sister."

The letters of introduction flew. Funny, they never met in high school. As students, my dad lived in town, my mother was a country girl, and a class ahead of him. It took a war to bring them together.

In Hawaii she flew over an active volcano, was given a coral by one scuba diving admirer, bought Hawaiian music and prints of Hawaiian girls wearing leis holding pineapples. Suburban Indianapolis had to feel like she was wearing handcuffs. Thus, the yellow painted floor. Something had to crack, only so much housework to satisfy the emptiness. She needed fulfillment and it finally came in the mail, a course in Handwriting Analysis. She stayed with it during our time in Indiana, through our many changes in Arizona and by my fifth grade year, she was a master, teaching a night class at the YMCA, and I have photos to prove it.

12. MONSTER-IN-LAW

Across the street from our Indianapolis home was a patch of land our neighbors, the Brinkmans, shared for gardening. My dad would return at times with armloads of lettuce and other greens.

One summer my grandmother, Zenith., my dad's mom, came to visit. Although she was in our house for at least a week, I do not recall any interaction. There seemed to be a distance set up, invisible, but real. One summer eve, as we sat at our kitchen table, the screen door open to the breeze, we were served a salad made from our garden's offerings.

I sat next to my grandmother. On her plate I saw one small, pale green worm inching its way along. Her fork was poised to engage with this exact area of her salad, only seconds away. My mouth dropped open and my eyes grew big.

I looked to my left, mouthing these words to my mother, "There's a worm on her salad!"

A negative shake of her head, she mouthed back, "Don't say anything!"

Stunned, I could not watch either the demise of the insect nor the response from my grandmother, who was oblivious to the addition to her dinner. I fully inspected my own plate, finished eating and retreated from the table in silence. I guessed my mother didn't like my grandmother very much, but I didn't know how deep this went, nor why.

That fall we returned to the small hometown where my parents grew up, Oblong, Illinois; still the home of my grandmother. Sleeping arrangements were being planned, and I wanted to be included.

Excited, I loudly and rudely declared, "I want to sleep with grandmother! Let me sleep with grandmother!"

Slap!

Full across my face, my mother's hand, never before touching me, left a hot red sting on my cheek. With tears flowing from my eyes, I ran from the room, down the stairs, and out the front door, confused at the cause, angry with my mother, and ashamed of my demanding behavior. I walked the circumference of this little spot surrounded by cornfields, and bitterly wished I could be anywhere but here.

What had I done? Was it my request or my delivery? Yes, I was being bratty, but was there more to this? I wondered.

– Chapter 3 –

13. ANOINTED

Just above my head, on a wall shelf, my mother had set the jar of varnish she had been using on a table in the basement, leaving me, a two-year-old, alone in the kitchen. Probably not the best idea. Also, the lid on the varnish was loose.

I could not reach it to take it down, but was able to turn it on its side, pouring the last of the gooey, slick stuff onto the top of my head on the hair that hung to my shoulders in a cascade of curls adhering them to my scalp in a surprising, pleasantly warm experience. Before and after photos show the missing locks and the short hair with a bow tied to a sliver of hair on top.

My mother's sister, thus my aunt, being a beautician, made it her mission in life to restore the curls with permanents, torturing a small child, leaving me with a fear of curly hair. The acrid smell of solution and the pink rubber things with tightly wound hair stayed with me.

Finally, however, the two of them, mother and sister gave up. I stayed a girl with short, straight hair.

I may have been a ballet dancer but for this fear. At seven, I was happily doing pliés at the bar, feeling lovely, and graceful, trying to copy the poses of my teacher, watching myself in the mirror. Then, at the start of class one afternoon, in bounced a curly headed redhead, buoyant in her pink tutu and matching slippers. My stomach turned. *Could you catch it, curly hair?* Hers was swirly, curly, piled on top of her head. *What if I caught it? From her?* You can catch a cold from a person. *Is curly hair caught, like a sneeze?*

How happy she was, spinning in circles! How terrified I was, in stunned silence! I had to quit. My mother never asked why. True, it was a mistake. I might be dancing at this very moment if not for that.

The fear returned just before my junior year of high school at Alhambra High. I, on my own, had decide to get a light perm, nothing major, just a little curl here and there. However, the incompetent person in charge of my hair left the solution on too long, leaving my hair fried.

My family had moved, and I was supposed to start at a new high school in the fall, only a few weeks away. No time to grow this out. I did not want to be the new girl who looked like a freak, so I decided to stay at the school where I was already accepted. First impressions can be ruinous.

This decision caused some difficulties. It meant nearly a mile walk from my house to the bus station in Glendale every morning and a quarter mile from the drop off to the school. It meant getting up earlier and getting home later. I was tired all the time, but I had avoided damaging my self-image and future dating opportunities.

I did go to the new school the next year, Glendale High, only a few blocks from my house. The yearbook photo from 1965 shows me with short straight hair, no curls, just like I wanted. The truth is it was great to be the new girl in school my senior year. The wait was worth it.

14. ESCAPE

One afternoon when I was three my mother decided that I needed a nap. The nap would happen on my parent's bed, on a white chenille spread, in their room with an open window, letting in a tender spring breeze sharing the air with the warm afternoon sun. It was just too inviting.

My mother removed my shoes, told me to sleep, shut the door and left me on my own with my first experience of temptation. Fresh and waiting for me to enter, just outside, was adventure. I went to the window, threw my right leg over the sill, and carefully moved my body out, holding firmly onto the wooden frame. It was thrilling.

But as I looked down, I realized that it was a long way to the ground below, much farther than I thought. I panicked immediately, pushing my feet, which were still in socks, against the siding, trying to get a hold, to shove myself back up, but my feet were sliding, and my fingers were hurting so I prepared myself to fall. Miraculously, it didn't happen.

Behind me I heard laughter. Someone was coming to save me, and I was gently lifted to the ground, saved by a kind neighbor who was entertained by my attempt to escape. My mother came down the steps and took me by the hand. Nothing was said to me. She returned me to the bed to take the nap I had avoided. Exhausted from my attempt at freedom, I fell asleep on the white chenille, in the warm sunlight, sinking into a dream on a cool breeze. Believing that, in the end, I would be rescued from myself.

15. IT WAS THE UNIFORM

When I headed out to play in the morning as a four-year-old, I would announce, "Boys! I'm out," at least that's what my mother told me. And they came running. I was second to the oldest, so maybe that's why. Ronnie was five. He wasn't handsome, but I was impressed with his clothes. His shirt was white with red embroidery at the shoulders, a real cowboy shirt. He wore jeans, leather chaps, boots and a holster for his pistol. I wasn't allowed to have a toy gun, but with my index finger I took aim and with my thumb I pulled the trigger. All we did was play cowboys, shooting and dying, over and over again.

It was lunchtime and all the kids headed home. Ronnie lived two houses past mine so we walked together.

At my house I turned to go in and he called after me, "Will you marry me?"

I was surprised, but didn't hesitate, thinking it might be good to get a commitment since no one else had asked me. I didn't want to be an old maid, like the card game, so I said," Yes."

Five minutes later I felt stressed and stupid. *What if I meet someone I like better?* But it was too late. I didn't know how to break an engagement. I was too inexperienced, not even knowing that a ring was required.

I purposely avoided him for a couple days, but then went to his house first thing after breakfast. I knocked, but no one answered. I knocked again harder. The door squeaked open, and I looked in.

I didn't see anyone, so I called, "Ronnie!" Again, "Ronnie!"

Still no one, so I stepped inside and called one last time. I must have bumped the door because it shut behind me. I decided to go home, but now I was locked inside Ronnie's house. My eyes welled up with tears, but quickly evaporated when I recalled the adventures of Goldilocks, so I went upstairs to his room.

On his shelf was his service station, a two-story wonder with gas pumps, service bays, a ramp, and an elevator. I set it on the rug and began filling the gas tanks of all his cars, putting a couple on ramps and using the elevator to get them back on the road. I didn't have anything like this, and I loved it.

I had pretty much mastered the skills required when I heard the thump of feet on the stairs.

Ronnie stomped into the room, hands on his hips, his head thrown back," Girls can't play with cars!"

That's not true. I just did. Obviously, they can. I got up off the floor, silently walked past him and left. It was over. I just needed to let him know, but how.

Two days later, he moved away. Problem solved.

16. A Very Short Ride

One fine spring morning my little sister, Claire, was allowed outside to play with me for the very first time. She was just past two and I was four. On her head she wore a knit cap with three small red balls on top, dressed for cold weather although the sun was shining, warming our little home.

As the responsible big sister, I planned to give her a ride on my new red tricycle. It was built for this, one large front tire, two small ones in the back with two steps up to the seat where I sat. She could stand on one of the steps and hold onto my waist for the ride.

Out she came, smiling, no longer a baby, ready to be a real kid. I showed her what to do and got in position. She stepped onto the back and took hold of me, but I was unprepared for the added weight and my feet skidded off the pedals. When that happened, the bike headed rapidly down the driveway out of my control as I kicked at the now spinning pedals, trying desperately to get my feet back onto them. As the bike neared the street, I heard the mighty blast of a truck horn and looked up to see a huge semi headed straight for the path ahead of us, the spot we were zooming toward.

My only control was the steering. I turned the handlebars hard right sending us into a ditch that bordered the front of the lot, alive, but face down in the dirt, my sister flying over me onto the grass. The trailing wail of the truck's horn flew past two little girls, one understanding how close we had come to sudden death and the other running crying to the house believing her big sister caused her to be hurt.

The morning was ruined. Claire wasn't allowed to play outside with me anymore, her roughneck sister who was the only one who knew the truth, that she was heroic, quick thinking and a very skilled driver, just totally unable to explain to her mother what had just happened.

17. THE HORRIBLE WOMAN NEXT DOOR

My neighbor had been watching me, but I didn't know it. She had a dog, Blue Anne, a large white Eskimo dog. Quite often I would stand at our chain link fence and talk to this large white fluff of a dog, stroking the small portions of fur that I could reach. I am sure that Mrs. Ray knew of my love for her dog.

So, a few days after Christmas she arrived at our front door with a Cocker Spaniel puppy for me. I was ecstatic. It was bedtime though, so my mother put Christy, my name for her, in a box in the kitchen and told me I would see her in the morning. Well, that is not what happened. I saw her for the last time as I went into my room. She was sitting in her box, watching me from the kitchen.

Here is the rest of the story, approximately sixty-three years later.

Out of curiously, I called my sister to ask a question. I couldn't recall playing together at all. I wanted to know more about our time as children, so I asked, "What do you remember about our evenings in Indianapolis? Did we play games, dolls or anything?

Her response was swift and abrupt, "I don't remember anything. I can't even recall what I did three weeks ago, so I couldn't possibly remember that."

"Well," I asked, testing her, "Do you remember the summer birthday party mother gave you for your sixth birthday since your actual birthday is the day after Christmas and you never had a party?"

"Yes, I remember that," she replied. "Do you remember that horrible woman next door? How horrible she was to mother! What was her name?"

What does this have to do with anything? "Charlene Ray."

"She gave you that puppy for Christmas and mother had to give it back! What a horrible woman!"

I felt my throat closing. Incredulous, I said, "She gave the dog back? That's not what mother told me. She told me the dog died during the night of distemper."

Her voice rose in irritation. "She didn't say that. Mother would never say that!"

"Well, she did," I said. That's what she told me, and I believed it!"

Conversation over. It was useless to ask her anything. No further questions for my sister.

As I considered the discrepancy in the two versions of my dog's disappearance, I thought back again to that time in my life. My rule then: I would allow my parents to provide for my needs.

That I accepted, but I forgot one important thing: *Who would take care of my heart?*

18. THE WHITE HOUSE

I am sitting at the window, waiting and watching for our old brown Oldsmobile to turn the corner. The restaurant review in *The Indianapolis Star* has invited my mother to a meal of home-cooked food. Images of golden, crisp fried chicken float in my head. Ready and waiting, I watch for my father while my mother bathes and dresses my little sister Claire. Finally, I see him turn the corner.

"He's home!" I announce.

In the kitchen, he sets his silver metal lunch pail by the sink and goes into the bedroom to change from the gray work pants smudged with ink from the newspaper where he sets type for the next day's news. This is how we know about the restaurant before the rest of the world. He reads it first.

Later, bouncing into the backseat, Claire and I discuss our orders. She wants only desert, "Cheerie Pie!" My mother turns to smile and wink.

"Stop that bouncing!" my father yells as we head into the sunset.

"How far is it?" Claire asks.

I watch out the window for the restaurant. I hear them say "The White House."

"Will we be eating with President Eisenhower?" I inquire hopefully.

"No," my mother answers and they laugh, but as usual I don't think I've said anything funny.

Annoyed and hungry, I return to looking out the window. We are passing lots of grimy factories and old service stations. It can't be here, I think. Rows of red brick apartment buildings come into view, their fences painted gray green.

There are no people out, but lots of lights are on in the little windows. I remember that one day last summer we passed here on the way to swimming lessons. A little girl my age was in her yard watching the cars go by. She saw me. Our eyes locked. I know she was wondering about me just as I was wondering about her. Could she be my friend? If we had a chance to meet, would she like me? Her face and skin were different from mine; would it matter? I would ask to hold one of her braids to see what it felt like. We would both laugh. Maybe she could be my friend.

We turn a corner, and we are there. It is a white house, but nothing like *The White House*. It has a front door, normal size, in the middle and two windows, one on each side of the door. White lace curtains hang in the windows. A narrow sidewalk leads from the street to the door. I see people inside eating dinner. My stomach rumbles. There is no place to park, and I wonder if there be a table left for us. A man looks out at us, his mouth full of food, probably mashed potatoes.

My dad parks a block away. I don't think I've ever been this hungry, so I'm hoping I'll remember my table manners and not embarrass my family.

"It must be seven o'clock," my mother comments.

The sun has separated day from night, and we have entered evening. We walk briskly, encouraged by the aromas coming from the restaurant.

I step onto the curb following my mother who is holding Claire's hand. Suddenly she stops. She is looking toward the door of *The White House*. I move in front of her to see. A family is standing at the door, intently reading a sign taped to the glass. It's strange, but I don't remember seeing a sign there moments before when the man was eating his mashed potatoes.

I feel suddenly cold. I button my sweater, glad that my mother made we wear it, but wishing we would hurry and go inside. My mother isn't moving. My dad stands there too, silent. They are watching the family at the door as they turn to walk away. The mother and father stare straight ahead. They look angry. The little girl hangs her head so low her chin almost touches her chest.

I don't understand. Then I realize, of course, the restaurant is full. I guess that means we won't be eating there either. I watch the girl pass me. In my mind, I reach out and touch her braid.

Instead, I feel her sadness and her parents' anger. Like steam from a pressure cooker, it hits me. I feel sick and ashamed without knowing why.

My father has gone ahead of us and is standing at the door reading. As we approach, he reaches out to open the door.

My mother puts her hand on the door, stopping him, "I want to read this."

I want to read it too, but I am in the third month of the first grade. My eyes follow left to right, looking for a word I know. The next to the last word… *not, not something*. I still don't understand.

My mother has read the sign.

My father tries again to open the door for us. "We aren't eating here," she says.

"Of course, we are," my father replies opening the door, but it is only partially open, for my mother has again placed her hand on it.

The people inside have stopped eating. Their eyes dart up and down with no place to land. Some are staring at their food. A few glance at us then quickly look away. My mother has shamed them. My father glares at her, but I know my mother, and we are not going in.

"If they can't eat here, we won't either. That family is just as hungry as we are!"

Holding her head high, she takes my hand and that of Claire. We turn and walk away. I feel hot. I know my face is red. I don't look back, but I imagine the people inside choking on their food. Perhaps they didn't know when they went in to eat that some people weren't welcome there. Perhaps they did, even though the sign wasn't there then. Someone inside made it is a hurry and taped it to the door when he or she saw the Negro family coming.

Back home in my place at the kitchen table, I hungrily slurp down a bowl of cold cereal and wonder what the little girl with the golden skin and thick braids was eating for her supper. I hoped she would look at me again next time I passed her way. I hoped she wouldn't hang her head, eyes down and walk away. I wondered; would she ever be my friend now?

19. THE FANNER 50

Christmas was approaching and although I had given up on Santa I still believed in presents.

Toy guns were big that year, realistic in multiple ways. The Fanner 50 was a silver, engraved beauty with a hammer that struck a button of gunpowder on a roll of caps easily inserted into the gun, releasing a whiff of smoke, the smell of fire and the thrill of power when the trigger was pulled. I had wanted a toy pistol since my younger days when I left the house yelling, "Boys! I'm out!"

Mostly I had given up on the idea, but this was new, and I wanted one. In the good old days of cowboy fights, I was armed only with my index finger and thumb, plus the noise of "*Ch…ch…ch,*" showing I had fired my weapon. My mother would not let me have a gun when I was five, but maybe she had changed her mind, now that the writhing bodies of little boys no longer spread across neighborhood lawns.

My announcement of, "You're dead! I killed you!" might have worried her somewhat.

Anyway, it was time to investigate. If there was a Fanner 50 for me there was only one place it could be hidden, in a small wall cabinet in my room very near the ceiling. To see it, I had to tilt my head backward, which meant it would be quite difficult to reach. Still, it could be done.

I got a chair, quietly, in case my mother might hear and become suspicious. It had a wicker seat. My foot might go through it, giving proof of my guilt, not to mention ruining the chair. I then got the biggest book I could find and centered it safely above the wicking, supported by the wood frame. I climbed up onto the pile of literature, but could tell it would not be high enough. I then got Audubon's large book of birds and several others to help me and built a leaning tower in my bedroom. Finally, I could reach the handle, but only on tiptoe and teetering, grabbing it quickly since I might fall. I peeked inside, and sure enough, there it was!

Thrilled, I silently replaced the books and chair. I was so happy. Suddenly, without warning though, my delight disappeared, and little pricks of guilt hit me. I felt like a thief hiding evidence of a crime. Still, who was to know? I struggled with my knowledge and waited for Christmas.

A surly sense of security replaced my usual anxious anticipation that Christmas morning, no rush to open presents this year. I glanced around, looking for a box the right size to hold a gun, but didn't see one. *Maybe a "Hold-up?"* I thought, just to surprise me. But no, suddenly within minutes it was over. *What was*

I going to do? It was here. I had seen it. What happened? I waited and waited for days. If I asked my mother about the gun, she would know I had snooped, ridiculously caught by my own curiosity. I had to know, "Mother, you know, uh, that, uh, Fanner 50 that, uh, was up in the closet?"

"Yes." Silence. Such torment she put me through!

"Uh, where is it?"

"Oh," casually responding, "Your aunt and I always switch your gifts, just in case someone snoops," she said, looking up, eyebrows raised.

She knew all the time. She knew but said nothing. My punishment was *waiting*! Waiting for Christmas, holding back my guilt! Even worse, I had to watch my cousin fire off his Fanner 50 while I sat in the dirt hitting caps with a rock.

20. FOLLOW YOUR NOSE

Nothing to do.

"Can I walk around the block?" I asked my mother.

"Which block?" she asked.

"Across the street…where the white house is."

"Alright," she agreed.

"But how do I do it?" I needed some guidance. I was four and a half years old.

"Just stay on the sidewalk, keep going and you will end up back here."

I could do that. I crossed the street and started walking. The houses were bigger than mine with lots of steps going to the front doors. These places were tall. My address was on Goode Avenue. Duplex B. I thought that meant that I lived on "Be Good Avenue."

I kept on walking, getting further and further away from home and a little nervous. I didn't see any people. I thought, *No one to help me if I get lost.* Still, I knew I wouldn't get lost.

I came to a corner and looked back. I had come a long way. I turned the corner, staying on the sidewalk. I kept on walking. I arrived at corner number two and began to run. At corner number three, I could see my house, only now I understood for the first time how very small it was.

Years later, one afternoon when I was seven, I decided to run away from home. For some reason I don't remember, I was angry at my mother, probably mutual.

"I'm leaving," I told her. "And I need a lunch." I expected a meal wrapped in a scarf attached to a stick which I would carry over my shoulder like I'd seen in a cartoon, but that's not what happened. She made a peanut butter sandwich, put it in a paper bag and handed it to me. I didn't want to ask her, but I needed some direction. The words fumbled out.

"Which way should I go?"

"Just follow your nose," she advised, unconcerned.

Not about to give her one inch of satisfaction for such an impossible suggestion, I started walking. I wondered if she was watching me. I wanted to know if she was worried. I hoped so. If I looked back and she was watching me, she would be at least a little anxious, but if she was not watching me, then she didn't care. I didn't want to know the answer in case she had already gone back in the house, and it didn't matter to her that a seven-year-old kid could get lost. So, I did not turn to see, although I felt the pull. I knew my nose would not fail me.

At the end of our street, there was a turn. Only one way to go, so on I went, pausing to eat my sandwich, which only served to make me thirsty. *Was that on purpose?* Again, the road turned. I had never been here before. Everything looked new. The street curved around to where it started. *Did this mean my escape had ended and the sidewalk would turn me back home?* There were some kids playing tag on a fresh green lawn.

A girl from my class yelled my name, "Hey! Want to play with us?"

Why not...I had nothing else to do.

After a breathtaking game of tag, we went inside to play Chutes and Ladders, a board game. It was new to me, sliding down, then climbing up, a very fun game.

About then I caught the aroma of food cooking. I looked up to see her mother in front of the stove preparing dinner.

Would this family like to have an extra kid?

Then her mother asked, "Do you know your phone number?"

Before I could think, I blurted out, "YE-7- 6355."

Yep, I knew my phone number.

As the game continued, smells rose from the kitchen as the sun slid down behind my back. I figured my mother was on her way.

Then, I heard the car idling outside and said, "Good-bye." Got in the car and went home.

That was it. That was all. No discussion. No apologies. Nothing to say.

I didn't have a problem with any of it though. I had been around the block before.

21. THE PUZZLE

The summer I was seven I was in Bible school of some sort as my parents often changed churches. I was in a large room with lots of other kids, cutting paper with a baby pair of scissors that did not work, so I took the real pair from the teacher's desk like the ones I used at home, and they worked just fine until she rudely grabbed them away from me. I waited until she let us go on a break and, by myself, escaped to a staircase which led to a small upstairs room where I found a puzzle and started putting it together.

I hadn't been there long when I heard footsteps on the stairs and three boys came into the room. I heard the oldest one who looked like he was twelve, say to the others, "I can show you how it's done."

Then he turned to me. "Lie down on the floor." There were three of them and only me, so I did what he asked.

"Watch," he told the other two. To me, he ordered, "Open your legs."

Then he lay on top of me and moved up and down above me. I didn't understand what he was trying to do, balanced on his arms, but he didn't touch me or hurt me. I felt uncomfortable, but not scared.

After only a minute or so, he got up and announced, "So, that's how you do it."

And they left.

More footsteps were coming up the stairs, harder and faster. By then I was back to working on the puzzle trying to dismiss the incident but confused by it. The woman from the scissor theft came in and looked hard at me. I felt my neck getting hot. She was big and I knew she was mean. Then she turned toward the center of the room and stared at the floor. I looked too. A wet spot was there, right where I had been lying, but I didn't do it. I hadn't seen it before. *What was that?*

Now her eyes bored into the back of my head. I wanted to escape from this hateful woman, from the room, from the church, but I kept on working on that puzzle, concentrating, holding myself tight, never looking up at her ugly face. Standing with my feet planted. I kept my fingers moving on that puzzle. I was stronger than her. Finally, she left, and I breathed a deep sigh, letting go of all I had held in, wanting to see the scissors planted in the middle of her back.

When my father came to get me, I climbed into the front seat next to him. As the car started to drive away, I opened the car door in a weak attempt at suicide, but he yanked my arm before I could fall and yelled at me, "Don't ever do that again!"

I decided I never would, and I didn't. I would never purposely hurt myself. Why would I? I figured there were others who were just waiting for their chance.

Later that year, my family was at a church picnic. It had recently rained and there were puddles everywhere. I was standing at the edge of one good-sized one. It was dusk and the light was dim, but there was a reflection at my feet, opposite me on the other side of the muddy bank.

It was the boy who? Who what? It was him. He was staring at me. I looked up, wondering why he was there. What did he want? Protected by mud, I still felt threatened. I didn't know how to react. I was confused. In great discomfort, I attempted a smile. *What? Did he like me?* He didn't smile back, but simply gave me a long stare, shrugged, turned and walked away.

22. THE HAND IN THE CASKET

My mother explained, "It will be easier for you to understand death if you see a dead person that is a stranger to you before you have to see the body of someone you love." This statement floated in the air until sometime later when she announced, "Get dressed (this meant good clothes) we are going to a funeral home."

I do not know if this was solely her idea or mine, as I was a curious child, but knowing I would actually be able to see a dead body sent little pricks up and down my spine. We arrived early in the evening, not yet dark, to my relief. My forehead was damp with sweat even though it wasn't warm weather.

Inside it was dark, cool, and silent, so very silent. The thick carpet swallowed my footsteps. I reached for my mother's hand. Time had stopped my real world, and I began to sense eternity.

Finally, we stood in the serene spot where it is too late for goodbyes. I could have touched the wooden box had I been brave enough or wanted to. I stood on tiptoe. There, right in front of me was a very large and creamy white hand. I shuddered.

This was not the whole show though. There was more to see. My mother lifted me up just long enough to get a glimpse of the entire body. She could only hold me up for a few seconds as I was six years old, not a little kid. I saw the clothing, a dress suit, black the kind men wear to church. I looked down at his face, not old or young. Thinking, I wondered, *Was he too young to die and why did he?*

Then it was done. Over. Survived. Breathing deeply, I relaxed. *Nothing to be afraid of now.*

We went home. Later, at bedtime, I thought about the day, testing myself for fear. I did not have any. The dead could not hurt me. I knew that now and I went to sleep.

23. THANKSGIVING

Our tires come to a slow stop, dusting the air behind them, Indiana, now a green memory. The land here stretches out in all directions, dry and powdery and brown. The sun, a worn gold pendant, hangs suspended, timeless against a dirty sky.

We have stopped in front of a small board house, once white, now a weathered gray. I climb from the backseat of the Oldsmobile and stand waiting for my mother. From somewhere nearby a child comes running up to me. She stops and stares. We are different in every way. She is younger than my seven years, but older in a way I don't understand. She looks at me in my polished oxfords and red and blue plaid school dress. She has no shoes and wears only a stained white cotton shift. Her face, streaked with lines of sweat and tears, is framed with blond hair twisted and matted into little ropes. I am her enemy, and she knows it. She glares at me with such fierce hatred that I almost fall backwards, but my mother grabs my hand pulling me toward her.

Our feet make no sound on the soft dirt. My toes are covered with dust by the time we reach door. My mother knocks and we wait. From inside, I hear the creak of a rocking chair, and a woman, large, but bend with age, opens the door wordlessly to let us in.

I blink into the darkness of the house. The room is empty except for the one chair, where the woman had been sitting. She tosses her hand toward an open doorway, motioning us on, then returns to her rocking once more. Still, all this and nothing has been said. I look back at her. She seems to be waiting for something.

The room we enter is lit by a window near the foot of a narrow bed. A man lies there on sheets worn thin by wear. We stand at the side of the bed looking down at him. He is old.

His hair lies in thin strands against his scalp. The skin on his face is transparent, yet the roundness of his cheek bones push it up, stretching its thinness like crisp parchment. He turns toward my mother, "So, you came after all?"

I sense a movement at the window, a sudden change in light. I move to see as they continue talking in hushed voices. On the glass, a smear from a child's hand quickly withdrawn traces across the steamed breath of a fading mouth print. What is left is my reflection looking back at me.

Outside, a broken tree stands, defiantly breaking the line of the horizon. The branches have long been gone. Only the trunk remains, one limb aiming upward. Lightning has struck the tree, I think, only I can't put the image of wind and rain into this scene of desolation.

My mother and the man talk quietly, but tension, a tightrope between them. Like a soldier, she stands stiffly at attention. A great distance lies between the pauses in their words. At one point he reaches up his hand seeking hers, but she doesn't take it. I can see pleading in his eyes. He is begging with a look. Her fingers open, but as she lifts her hand, his face changes to a smirk. Her hand drops to her side, and she turns to me, "We need to go now." I leap the distance between us and grasp her hand. We pass the old woman, letting the screen door slam behind us.

Kneeling on the backseat, I watch the road unwind like a ribbon tossed away. The shack fades in the distance as our car weaves homeward. I lean my chin on the back of my mother's seat to ask, "Who was that man?", but I change my mind when I see her tears. I figure I already know.

What I do not know is how it came to this between them, but I learn and begin to understand. She was his first-born child. He named her Jesse, the name for the boy she was supposed to be. Eleven months later she rocked her brother's cradle. She seemed to draw his wrath, so she found a hiding place under the stairs. By the age of eleven she was the leader of a small band of soldiers who maneuvered under her command. More than one night the army defended their mother against the father made unrecognizable by alcohol. The younger ones, under orders, surrounded their mother, while the eldest flayed him with a broom, shortly defeated, he would retreat as he cursed this homegrown "Japanese Army!"

I was in my twenties before I learned about "Kansas." The wind was battering the windows that day, sending a chill into the room. My arms were full of kindling for the fire I was starting in the fireplace when she began.

"My dad moved us to Kansas after his store failed," she said. "I had to sneak out every night, well past midnight to take firewood from the neighbor's stacks. The place we had was just a cabin with big holes between the logs. I thought we would freeze to death there."

I could see she was distraught with the memory of her theft, apparently not seeing it as it did, an act of conscience.

"You didn't really have any choice."

"I know," she replied.

I didn't ask for any more information.

Many years had passed, and my mother was dying. In September she developed pneumonia, and her weight dropped to 104 pounds. By November, she had not only resigned herself to death, but seemed to be hoping for it. On the night of Thanksgiving, I went to the hospital. The nurse at the desk looked up to acknowledge me, giving me permission for this late visit with an understanding nod.

My mother is sleeping, but restless under the eternal nightlight above her bed. Her forehead tightens into a frown.

Gradually she senses my presence and opens her eyes. Looking at me intently she asks, "Why can't I die?"

I am not sure I am qualified to answer this question. "How can I know that?" I ask.

She starts blaming it on her ancestry, the sturdy Scottish grandparents, and the English immigrants who sired us all. Apparently, they too had outlived their time.

It seems silly and I smile at her. She sees it too. She squeezes my hand and falls back asleep.

By two a.m. even the straight-backed chair can't keep me awake. She frowns and mumbles. She is reaching upward, motioning, pleading to God, "Let me go…let me go….let me die."

I touch her hand, "Mother?"

Quickly, she pulls her hands to her chest. She seems embarrassed. I know of no other way to help her, so I ask, "Maybe God has something you need to finish?

She looks puzzled.

"Is there someone you hate or haven't forgiven?"

She ponders that, hesitating, "I don't know of anyone."

We have come this far for some reason. "What about your father?" I suggest reluctantly.

A long sigh escapes, "Oh-h-h him."

She does not see me. She is collecting, sorting… I wait.

I know so little about them, her and her father. I imagine her hands holding the things I do not know. She grips each bitter relic; clenching, unclenching, again, and again and again until finally surrendering she says, "I can…I will forgive him."

At this moment I see her in a vision. She is standing at the far end of a deeply furrowed field. The soil is rich and dark; the furrows deep, ready for planting. Behind her the sky swirls and moans. A storm is coming. Her hand is at her forehead, as if she is looking into a bright light, still trying to see me so far away. As I watch, I become aware that she has changed. She stands tall, outlined against the darkened sky. I see her as she once was, her image stored in a box of family photographs. She is young again.

24. DOUBLE BUBBLE TROUBLE

It seemed like a good idea, to sell rocks. They were beautiful, especially when it rained. Who wouldn't want one of these rounded marvels? I piled as many I could into my wagon and started going door to door. Not interested at the first house, but I saw a woman hanging up clothes in the backyard of the house next door so I dragged my rock collection in her direction.

She didn't want any either. How was I ever going to make any money? A seven-year-old can't get a job so what else could I do?

Her husband came out the backdoor, "Want a piece of gum?"

"Yes," I said, following him to his car.

"Get in," he motioned, so I opened the passenger door and slid in. He handed me a piece of Double Bubble gum. I was reading the joke when I looked over at him. He had unzipped his pants and was holding his thing. I never had seen that before, but I had seen my mother prepare chicken, and this looked like a chicken neck to me. I thought it was time to leave before things got worse. This was already bad. I opened the door and scrambled out.

He called after me, "Don't tell anybody."

His wife was still hanging up clothes. *What kind of woman does that?* She must have known. I left my wagon with all the rocks and ran home. The first thing I did, of course, was tell my mother.

The next day she took me to the doctor.

"I'm not sick," I protested, "Why are we here?"

"Just a check-up"

The doctor, a woman one, came in. "We need you to hop up onto the table." Which I did.

She made me take my pants off and lie down. I was scared. *What are they doing to me?*

"Put one foot here and one here." My legs were apart, and my feet were cold on metal things. *Why are they doing this?* My mother's face looked scared, more scared than me. *Why is she so scared?*

The doctor stopped touching me and took off her gloves. "I see no evidence of penetration."

She said, "You can sit up now."

I just wanted to go home. I felt funny, like I was going to be sick. I didn't understand.

What does "penetration" mean?

– Chapter 4 –

25. A Very Long Ride

I would need a dictionary. I was certain of that, as there was not one at my house. I had to pull together my courage to ask Mrs. Hogan, my third-grade teacher if I could borrow one for two weeks. The plan was to learn as many words as possible and actually read the entire book as we drove from Indianapolis to Glendale, Arizona for Christmas vacation. Tucked under the driver's seat, the dictionary was safe and easily reached. With me I also had a small, light blue spiral notebook to record our journey.

I started reading immediately as my father headed for the highway. Symbols on the first pages made no sense to me so I went to the first words, A, an, etc.

As I read, the movement of the car and the bouncing of the tires on the road began to bother my stomach. I got as far as aardvark, then pushed the dictionary back under the front seat, knowing half of my plan had just failed. Turning to the journal, I began to write. For some reason it didn't bother me in the way reading did, but it did make me tired, and as nothing had happened yet, I had nothing to say. I did know that a capitol letter was on the first word and the last word was followed with a period.

We must've driven until late into the night because I barely remember struggling to walk into our motel room, crumbling into a sweet sleep somewhere in Missouri, which as I now know is just over a five-hour drive from Indiana.

About mid-morning the next day, heading south, we came across signs promoting The Onondaga Caves. I made a request, "We have to stop and see the caves! We'll never have a chance to do this again," relentless in my own way as the billboards appeared and reappeared every few miles down the road. Maybe my parents were ready for a break or maybe they knew that kids needed adventure, but stop they did, and bought the tour tickets.

The caves were chilly, so I put on my sweater. I brought it even though I didn't believe I would use it in Arizona. For the last few days, I had made sand mountains in my sandbox, trying to create the treeless, desert world facing me. Here in the caves, the echoing sound of dripping water droplets was refreshing. I also learned two new words, stalactite and stalagmite, but I couldn't remember which went up and which came down, completely forgetting to refer to my available reference book under the front seat, the first evidence of my ambition exceeding my dedication, a common occurrence throughout my life.

On we went to Oklahoma, me working on my sticker book, pasting as I recall, breeds of dogs on the appropriate spots.

I remember the dignity of a German Shepherd but soon a page with horses intrigued me, and I carefully glued down a rearing golden Palomino stallion, convinced that in Arizona I would surely have a horse like that of my own.

As nothing much was happening, I began documenting our meals, mostly mine and usually desserts. Somewhere along the way, most likely Texas, we stopped at a little diner. It was late afternoon. The land around was yellow brown and grassy. Far off, in the distance, a train was passing, too far away to hear its metal wheels. I asked my father for a quarter to play the juke box and for the first time I heard Johnny Cash's deep voice sing *"Ring of Fire"* as I watched the departing train. Why I choose that song, unknown to me before, held an image in my mind forever. His deep voice, the imagined rumble of train wheels and the sun, as it lingered for one stupendous moment left a melancholy fondness within me.

On to New Mexico. I awoke to the sound of rain pattering on the roof of our car, and with it the sound of thunder in the distance. It was still dark and since I had never been awake at such an early hour, I asked, "Where is the sun?"

"It hasn't come up yet."

"Well, why not?"

"It is too early. You are up before sunrise."

My little sister still slept beside me.

"When will it come up? What if it doesn't? How do you know it will?"

"It always does."

"But what if today it doesn't?"

They laughed at me, and I shut up. Anxiously braced on my knees, holding onto the back of the seat, I waited and watched out the window for the sunrise. When it finally threw its flames onto the earth, I was stunned by its beauty. Every drop of rain glistened in the light. I sighed in relief, turned around and waited for breakfast somewhere in New Mexico, but as we made our way through the mountains my father slowed to look at a man standing by the side of the road.

"What was he doing here," I wondered?"

Through my mom's now open window, my dad asked him some questions. We learned he was a soldier on leave, heading home for Christmas.

"Get in!" my father told him, and I scooted to the middle of the seat, trying not to touch the dripping wet soldier but waking my sister with my move. I had never heard my father talk about the army, but he advanced into a story about his time in Okinawa, a mess sergeant in a war. As my father was usually silent, this odd meeting showed me his history. The wet stranger and my father had a bond. Finally, we stopped to let him out and as he left, he thanked us and gave me a wide smile. In my heart I felt a great and generous thing had happened, glad that we had stopped to help a hero. As soon as he left, my father retreated into his silent world.

Down the road in Gallup, I saw my first horses. Sure, I had seen them in Indiana but these were horses with cowboys attached. There were Indians too, the women wearing purple velvet skirts. I could see their boots and silver belts. We didn't stop there though so all I got was a quick look as we passed through the town. We had to be getting close to Arizona.

Once we crossed the border, my dad took what he must've thought would be a great shortcut down the road going through the Salt River Canyon.

"Boy! That's a long way down," I remarked, as we navigated along a winding two lane road above a canyon far below us, my dad steadily grasping the steering wheel, my mom looking at her hands, retreating from the view. Back in Indianapolis, she would have nightmares of our Oldsmobile careening over the side, smashing its way to the bottom of the canyon but that didn't happen.

"How much further?" I asked, as we zipped past one last mountain range.

"There's gold in that mountain," my father announced, trying to distract me from questioning time and distance.

"A dying miner gave someone a map to where it was hidden but no one has ever found it. It is still there somewhere in that mountain."

"We should stop and look for it," I stared out at the passing landscape.

"It is much further than it looks," my father said. "Distance here is different."

Suddenly, we were on a flat road leading us through miles of billboards, gas stations and motels. My visions of gold turned to my Golden Palomino. Remembering the rearing stallion, poised on his two hind legs, I tried to picture myself in the saddle and became concerned that I might not be able to hold on. I became worried that I would fall off the back of my horse. I thought about that all the way through Phoenix as the light faded into dusk.

The last thing I saw before drifting off to sleep was a neon sign for a motel, an exhausted Indian, feathers in a band on his head, a loin cloth on his hips, asleep on his horse.

I was in Arizona. Would it be my new home? Would I get a stallion?

26. LOST IN ARIZONA

In the middle of my third-grade year, right after our Christmas trip, my family left Indiana and moved to Arizona. My father had been laid off from his job as a linotype operator at *The Indianapolis Star*, but fortunately for him, *The Arizona Republic* had the same owner, and he was able to keep his job by moving to Phoenix.

My grandmother's two-bedroom house at 309 West B Street already housed three people, my aunt, who had left her husband, and her two daughters, my cousins. They had the second bedroom with bunk beds and my aunt slept with my grandmother in her room. What was left was a small room that had been a carport. My parents slept there on a hideaway bed and my little sister had the couch in the living room. I had a green army cot wedged against the wall in a corner of the family room. It was impossible to find any comfortable position for sleep in its shallow nest and my only companion was Growly, my Teddy Bear. It was all there was, and I was left to deal with it.

It didn't take long for me to figure out my place in this new life. One afternoon I was watching my favorite TV show when my cousins came in and one of them changed the channel. She didn't even ask. She just did it. That wasn't fair, so I told my mother, and she said, "They get to choose. They were here first," and that ended it. *No taking turns? They were here first. What!* I felt like I had lost everything.

Immediately, I walked out the door and I kept on walking until I was too hot and too tired to go on. I did the same thing every day for weeks. Nobody asked where I was going, and nobody asked where I had been. When I wasn't wandering the neighborhood, I stayed in a hiding place on a brick fence between my grandmother's house and the neighbor's where I could stare at their swimming pool with its shimmering blue water, as sweat poured down my face and my insides filled with rage. There I could power up.

Adding to this, my mother had no time for me. Every day she sat with my grandmother at the kitchen table. If I tried to interrupt, I was shooed away. I never cried though. I just added it to my list.

My older cousins, Pat and Sue besides watching their TV shows, stayed in their room with a closet full of games and toys, which never once included me or my sister. We did take turns for one thing though, doing dishes. Not fair either. There were two of them to do the dinner dishes for 1, 2, 3, 4, 5, 6, 7, 8 people, but the same job was mine, without help because my little sister was too young, or too small, or whatever. So, after the dishes were done by a barely eight-year old, me, I would return to my small spot on the hot brick wall, where I could simmer and reload my internal arsenal that would eventually explode.

27. ONE DIVIDED INTO TWO = TROUBLE

It happened. I am not making this up.

It was afternoon recess, and it was hot. No shade anywhere. In Arizona, May weather wasn't like Indiana, and I was miserable. With sweat on my forehead, loitering at the edge of the playground with nothing to do, I saw my cousin, Paul, who was eight, like me, only three months younger.

He and two other boys were behind the fence at the baseball diamond on the far end of the playground. One was pitching, one was batting, and Paul was watching.

My feet started moving. I was walking, but I didn't mean to. It was like someone else was inside me making me go. I walked, but it wasn't me walking.

What was this?

I came to the fence and leaned up against it, putting my fingers through the chain link. I made sure the boys were watching, and I pulled up my dress. I felt shocked.

I would never, ever do this! They could see my new red panties!

Someone else did this, did it on purpose.

Whoever it was, it wasn't me.

I walked slowly around the fence and lay down on the grass. Maybe the pitcher or the batter knew what to do. Whichever one it was, moved up and down, like the other boy from before but this time I felt something. I closed my eyes.

Just when I started to float away, somebody strong grabbed me by the collar of my dress and fiercely yanked me to my feet, totally lifting me off the ground. He, who I figured was a teacher, was breathing heavily, muttering threats I could not clearly understand, dragging me on his left and Jorge on his right. Whatever he was saying was lost in the sound of our feet scraping the dust of the playground.

I knew I was in big trouble, but I really didn't do anything. Who would believe that?

By now *"she"* was gone. Of course, leaving me to tell my story.

At the Principal's Office, I was thrown into a chair by the door, the office staff glancing up. The boy was taken in first. I waited, steadily holding my eyes on the floor by my feet.

I didn't look at anyone. I didn't want anyone to see me, so I didn't look, only at the floor.

I wanted to be invisible.

What would I say?

What could I say?

This wasn't like me. I never got in trouble.

I followed the rules. I was polite.

I didn't lie but now I would have to.

After a long, long time, I heard a door open, and Jorge's feet passed by me. I was next.

In the Principal's office, I looked up at him, only one short look. He leaned forward in his chair.

He had a kind face. I felt better, but I only looked once.

"What happened?"

Here is where I lied. I had to.

"He knocked me down."

A long silence. I still looked down, this time at my hands. No other questions. I was free to go, but not to the classroom and math. I was sent home early. Directly home. No getting anything from my desk. That was it.

Whew! What a relief!

But it was a long, slow, hot walk home. The sidewalk felt like fire under my feet.

Did anyone see what I did?

Who was watching? Did they know?

Did my teacher know?

Did the principal call my mother?

My family had recently moved out of my grandmother's house to a dumpy little shack a few blocks away. Once home, I collapsed on my bed. I had a bed now. It was large and located on a porch next to the kitchen, not really a bedroom, just a place to put a kid.

I slept and I slept. I didn't wake up to eat or talk. I was sick, miserably sick. For weeks, I lay feverish, missing the entire last month of the third grade because of measles. Lucky me! The angels had protected me again. I did not have to go back to school. I did not have to try to explain or see accusing eyes. Nothing was ever said.

Did my mother know? Would "she" come back?

28. REMEDIAL MATH

I was given the news, finally, that a decision had been made. Because of my bad behavior I wouldn't be a fourth grader, but that wasn't the reason they gave me, even though I knew the truth. I would skip fourth grade entirely.

Why, I wondered. *Was I too tall, too smart or too much trouble?* I was told that my reading level was well above fourth grade, so, on that basis I would go to the fifth grade.

Did they forget about math?

One hot summer morning the doorbell rang. There stood my third-grade teacher, Mrs. Leon, one person I had never expected to see again, nor did I want to. My mouth open, unable to speak, I stood there. Inside I was shaking, terrified, expecting to be accused of something I could not begin to understand, like a leaf holding onto a broken branch, certain to fall.

"Oh, come in," my mother approached from behind me, and greeted her warmly.

"You can work together in the family room."

Work on what? I was wondering.

Paralyzed, something inside me rose up and tightened, a choking feeling left me unable to speak.

Then it became clear. We started the time's tables. 2x2=4, 2x3=6 and on and on.

Once a week I tried to think in numbers. I had to memorize them, all of them. I didn't need her. I could have done this all by myself.

The stress of having Mrs. Lowe next to me kept the playground scene repeating in my head, like a merry-go-round that you can't get off of. I was mixing up the 6's, 7's and 8's. I was good with the 9's, 10's and 11's, but forget the 12's. All summer this went on, terrified of the past, worried about the coming year I would be a fifth grader.

Could I do it?

Why did my mother hire her? Just to terrify me.

Well, it worked. I feared her coming every… single… time. I held myself steady, my spine made of steel, all the time feeling my heart pounding so loudly, I thought for sure she would hear it. Math, I never got it.

29. FROM BOOKS TO BOMBS TO BASEBALL

I was almost seven when I started first grade. I was the tallest, so Mrs. Behrman put me in the last seat in the first row so I wouldn't block the view of the little kids. I caught on to reading like I did swimming, learning to float like a swan. I quickly ran past Sally, Dick and Jane, and was allowed to read books from the closet at the front of the room. Whatever was happening in the class didn't include me. I was reading like a stray dog, hungry for those delicious words.

The first word I learned was bed. The word looked like a bed. Two boards, one at the head (the line on the b), and one at the foot (the line on the d). The b had a pillow and the d, a rolled-up blanket. It all made so much sense to me. By December I was warm and snuggly in my desk, drinking in language, book after book after book.

I remembered this about myself and began to feel better about the coming year in fifth grade, having skipped the fourth. It would be a chance to read many more books. That fifth-grade year

I read *"Green Mansions"* by Hudson, and the biographies of Lincoln and Madame Curie. I was convinced that if I learned about the mistakes made by these people, I would avoid making any mistakes in my life. Lincoln didn't make any mistakes that I knew about, but Madame Curie sure did. She sacrificed herself for science. If I became a scientist, I decided, no sacrifices for me.

That same year we heard something about Cuba and started practicing in case a bomb was dropped on us.

How did we know about this?

We got to see a film about Japan. It showed the people who lived there when America bombed their city. We saw people burned black. We got to see others with skin peeling off their bodies, their faces scabbed, eyes blinded by a flash of light.

At any moment, the school alarm bell would ring. We were supposed to cover our eyes with our right arms and use our left wrists to hold our heads on our necks, then tuck ourselves into balls and roll under our desks. Wait for the flash and then the impact.

One time we left school and went across the street to an empty irrigation ditch next to a field of carrots. As we left, I helped myself to a carrot.

The cartoons after school were sing-song tunes replaying our school routine for "Duck and Cover." I tried to convince my parents that we needed a bomb shelter.

"I want to use the shovel," I told them. "We need a bomb shelter."

They laughed at me, but it didn't matter. I would have to do it myself, so, I went out to the storage room, got the shovel and began to dig. I pushed the tip of it into the spot where I thought we would have enough space for a room underground, but it was more than I could do. The ground was too hard to make any real progress. At one inch down I put the shovel back in the storage room and went inside to watch "Rocky and Bullwinkle."

Boris and Natasha were the Russian enemies who were trying to bomb us, but Rocky always fixed it. I quit worrying about sudden death or radiation sickness.

I did have a bad dream though. I saw my sister running from the burning house, our parents still inside trapped. I, however, was saved by Rocky, the Flying Squirrel.

Besides showing children photos of Hiroshima victims, my fifth-grade teacher, turned on the TV when spring came and we all got to watch baseball games during class, while outside on breaks the boys played the game.

One kid, Rick, was hit in the stomach by a fly ball during lunch recess. He sat next to me smelling like sweat and dirt, with his head bent down, holding his stomach, moaning in pain. Barely able to raise his hand, in his weakened voice, he asked, "May I go to the nurse?"

Of course, I thought, he can go. Look at him.

But Mr. Butler said, "No."

What? Stunned, I looked at Rick.

After a moment, he pushed himself from his desk and staggered from the room. We were all silent. I couldn't even look at my teacher.

Why was he even here?

It wasn't long before we heard an ambulance.

He's dead, I figured. But after two weeks when I hadn't heard, I asked my mother.

"Uh…what happened to Rick?"

"He had appendicitis. His parents moved him to another school."

"Oh."

Hmmm, I thought. I bet Mr. Butler is in big trouble. I would test my theory.

The next day, bored by the drone of the television and suffering from the stifling heat, I bravely raised my hand.

"Mr. Butler, may I go to the nurse? I don't feel well."

"Okay," he said without hesitation, and immediately wrote me a pass.

It worked. Now, I had freedom. I didn't want to push my luck, so I only used this tactic occasionally, but as often as I could during Geography. Man was it boring. People in China planting rice, or was it Japan? The Boring Sea…the rivers in France, the ponds, the puddles, etc. I could barely keep my head from falling to my desk. I needed a nap.

"Mr. Butler, may I go to the nurse? I feel sick."

"Yes."

I took the pass.

The school nurse was the nicest person in the world. She let me rest on the cot. I fell asleep.

The dismissal bell woke me. Feeling refreshed and relaxed I went home. It was heavenly.

Poor Rick. Lucky me.

30. PURE AND SHINY, FOR NOW

"You wear a robe, walk down into a tank of water, hold your nose and fall backwards," Max said. "You come out pure and free from sin."

He should know since he was the preacher's son.

The Sunday school kids were all talking about getting baptized.

"What keeps you from drowning?" I asked.

"Oh. The minister won't let you drown. He just dips you into the water, that's all. It only takes a second," Max told us, promoting our salvation.

Pure and spotless, free from sin. Sounded good to me.

But for how long? Could I stop having bad thoughts, wanting things that were out of reach, or daydreaming when I should have been paying attention?

It was doubtful.

Another problem. You had to accept Jesus as your Lord and Savior and give your life to Him.

I could do part one, but give my life to anyone? No! I was in charge of my own life. Thank you! Hands off!

These worries became a constant source of anxiety, especially as the big day was fast approaching.

Who would know anyway? If I lied.

Who would know? Of course, God.

This was not a simple matter. And I would know. I would always know that I had lied to get into heaven.

Does it work that way? I didn't just want to pretend to be good. I wanted to BE GOOD, like the street I lived on before, in apartment B on Goode Avenue.

I was meant to be a good person.

Could I do it alone? It had worked so far. Maybe I could even be a saint? The Catholics had them. Did our church recognize saintly children? I had managed just fine for twelve years.

Why would I need help now?

About this time, my mother heard of a new religion, one predicting the return of Christ.

"You get a number on your forehead," she informed me. "There is one government for the whole world and there will be world peace."

Sounded good to me. I wouldn't need that bomb shelter. So, I began to pray.

Prayer had worked before.

#1 When I saw a dog all alone near a field and my father said if it was there on our way home it could be mine. We were on the way to church then, so I prayed all the way there, the whole time I was there and all the way back to where the dog was still waiting. When I opened the door, in she jumped. Prayer answered.

#2 When my mother's car was trapped behind a fire truck on a narrow bridge and a pole on the truck swung loose threatening to slam into the windshield and impale her, I was supposed to duck down behind her seat. I didn't. I watched its shaky, random swing, the pole loosening and sliding toward us. I prayed then and watched it bounce off the bridge support and fall into the river below. Prayer answered.

Here was my chance.

"Please God, let me be alive when Jesus comes back. That's all I want. Just that. Please let me stay alive to see it happen. I don't care if I'm really old. Just let me be here when it happens. Thank you, God."

I let it go, feeling certain of my inclusion in the coming event. My heart felt pure, and I hadn't even been baptized.

A singular thought followed this prayer.

Could it be possible that God, who gave me life, would want good things for me, maybe even better than I could do on my own?

I fought this idea. I was just fine. I didn't need anyone but myself. But a tenderness came over me and my heart softened. I decided to be baptized.

When I did rise from the water, dripping wet, soaked, head to my rocking heels, I felt held, secure, protected.

Did anyone see a glow of light around me?

31. PRIVILEGES

My aunt Berta was a den mother for the Cub Scouts and because I spent so much time with my cousin, Paul, I had the privilege of attending a meeting. The first thing I learned in the first ten minutes was leg wrestling.

Leg wrestling, if you have never tried it, is done on the floor, with the two participants side by side, heads in opposite directions, hips next to one another. Count one, legs up; two, legs up, three, grab your opponent's leg with yours and yank back, flipping the other kid over, leaving him stunned, but unhurt.

I was a strong eight-year-old and tall for my age, both advantages when it came to this. None of them would challenge me more than once, so I guess I was the champ. The rest of the meeting I have forgotten, but the general atmosphere was exciting, plans for camping, hiking, fishing, etc.

One Saturday Paul was sent to the barbershop for a haircut, and I happened to come along. As we entered, the gentlemen in the chairs were brashly discussing seemingly important topics using words I had never heard before. When they saw me, the place fell silent. I thought it odd that my presence had caused this to happen, but let it go as I headed to the stack of *"Boy's Life"* magazines at the back of the room.

As Paul's hair fell to the floor with the click of scissors, I entered a whole new world, one of pogo sticks, boomerangs, hunting knives, binoculars, canteens, bows and arrows, oars, and sling shots, discovering things I had no knowledge of before. I kept this information as a profound belief in equality, looking forward to the day I would be in Girl Scouts, experiencing the tough outdoor life.

Finally, in seventh grade, it was time. I became the troop's secretary, keeping weekly minutes on Wednesday afternoons for our thirty-minute meetings during which nothing ever happened worth writing about.

Who attended? Their names. How much money in dues did we collect?

Some days I could barely do it, getting a headache from boredom.

"When are we going camping?" I asked.

"We don't do that," replied Mrs. Ample. "We are going to plant rose bushes…in front of the school…soon…very soon."

For the one year I endured the organization. We did crafts, flower arranging, had a few ice-skating lessons and sold cookies, but when I pulled my wagon up to one house, I heard a man yell,

"If it's another one of those damn Girl Scouts, I'm going to kill her!"

I did a U-turn toward home faster than you could say "Thin Mint."

On Christmas Day my gift was a Girl Scout uniform, lovingly given by my mother who did not know I was slipping from the grasp of the Girl Scouts week by week. I wore it for only one occasion. It stayed hanging in my closet, a crisp green reminder, until eventually it disappeared, gone and thankfully forgotten.

The privileges I had considered to be mine had not appeared. I did not understand the why of the differences between the scouts. My mother's attitude showed me something though.

"Andrea, you must never beat a boy at a game. You need to let them win."

When I heard that I thought, s*he doesn't know me very well.*

I would never succumb to self-inflicted losses when I had every bit as much strength and power as one of them.

Who was she? What was wrong with her?

Of course, like all girls, I grew up and learned the phrase, "Boys will be boys."

What did that mean? That they can do whatever they want?

Is there a similar saying, "Girls will be girls?"

What might that mean?

I would fix it. Girls will be courageous, powerful and equal to boys.

They must be. The world didn't need more cookies. We needed inclusion.

My mother eventually proved to be somewhat aligned with the feminist movement, but it took years. I was a sophomore in college and home for the weekend when she asked me to decorate a box for a church luncheon. It was a competitive event, not only for the contents but for the illustrations. She wanted me to draw women burning their bras.

Thrilled with her change in attitude, I did my best cartooning. Each side of the box had a campfire with a woman holding a bra on a stick, just like you would roast a marshmallow. Short of time, I did not get to put finishing touches on the lid, and she ran out the door.

Good things can happen unexpectedly- her box sold for the most money!

In my head I heard cheers from the church ladies, enlightened and hopefully ready to teach their daughters and granddaughters to hang tough, knowing times have changed.

32. BECOMING A GIRL

My cousin was like a brother to me. With him, I could do boy stuff.
I learned to shoot marbles but was locked out of his room when his friends played. I lay on the carpet in the hall, trying to see under the door, hearing the *click*, *clack* of striking marbles. I wasn't angry. I understood. He was just afraid I would show him up in front of his friends.

We could arm wrestle, my only opponent. Girls did not do that. We shot off firecrackers under glass bottles but ran as fast as we could to safety. On the way home from school, we waded in the irrigation canal, hearing the rush of water headed to Arizona fields. The Mexican kids joined us, telling us to watch out for La Llorona, the ghost of a woman hunting for her drowned children that she murdered. I tucked my skirt into the legs of my underwear and waded in with the rest of them. On Sundays, we had long hot walks to the Chinese market, the only place to buy anything on a Sunday in Glendale. We bought candy cigarettes, wax lips and

Laffy Taffy, pointing to what we wanted as the store owner spoke no English.

Under the Cottonwood trees, their white snow falling on us, we played with roly-poly bugs, as the cicadas sang their anthems. One time we found a horny toad and let him go. Another day a red racer looped around our wrists until he too was released.

Something had to be done. My mother and my aunt secured a class which included my sister and my two cousins, Sue and Pat. "How to Act Like a Lady" may have been what it was called. I wanted to go only because my cousins would be there. They went for enhancement, me, for intervention. Walking gracefully was necessary. Going up stairs without clumping was practiced. Three steps up, a platform, then three steps down.

"Do not look at your feet!" barked the woman in charge, the tight bun on the back of her head stiff like the rest of her.

I had to watch my feet. At age twelve I wore size 9 ½. If my feet didn't fit the steps the whole thing would topple. Well, I did it!

That's over with, I thought relieved, but no, we had to repeat the stair exercise with a book balanced on our heads. My cousins both did just fine, but I had to hold my arms out to the side for balance, probably looking like a penguin.

That was not the end of it. No one else had eyebrows like mine. I had never noticed that they grew, nearly touching, just above my nose.

What difference did it make?

Well, I guess it was important for a girly look, so I had to start plucking my eyebrows, and it stung. The intense pain brought tears to my eyes.

What is wrong with people? I was fine just as I was before.

Did I become more feminine? I guess, but it wasn't easy.

Did boys need to become more masculine?

Nope! It was all built into their lifestyle. Still, if kickboxing had been there for girls, it would have been no more painful than tweezers yanking out hairs from between your eyes, pain streaking across your forehead, with tears running down your face.

33. THE INCIDENT AT THE SILVER POOL

My cousins and I were going swimming at the Silver Pool, a public pool full of kids all summer. I was the last one out of my mother's car and just as I slammed the door and started walking, I suddenly felt someone touching me. These hands pressed against my chest, then moved down my body all the way to my legs. It happened in an instant. I turned to see a man running away.

My mother had just backed the car up to the exit, her face turned toward the busy street. I paused and watched her leave. *Did she see what had just happened?*

At home later I asked her. Yes, she had seen him do that.

"Why didn't you do something?" I asked, disturbed that she had dismissed the incident so willingly.

"I figured you'd be fine in the pool with the other kids."

"But you didn't do anything about it," I confronted her.

"What could I do?" Her excuse.

What could I do? I wondered. Not count on her to protect me, for sure. That I could do.

34. FLUTELESS

The name of the teacher who passed out musical instruments was Mr. Honey. He wore round glasses, had sandy brown hair that flipped just over his forehead and the kind of face that made you believe you could trust him. I was offered a clarinet, but my mother sincerely believed that the clarinet would push my teeth forward requiring dental work to restore their position, so no clarinet for me.

Still, I was intrigued by the lovely, black, slender form, the reed at the mouthpiece with attachments for fingering, but after watching Priscilla Williamson prepare to demonstrate its sound, the licking, sucking and drooling ruined the clarinet for me.

What was next was the flute. No slobbering to prepare it for playing, plus it was beautiful, a silver hollow reed. The sound was pure, not emitting random squeaks like the clarinet did on occasion, leaving your ears quivering and your eyes watering. Besides it felt good to hold. The keys had soft little pads to hold them tight. The hollow on the keys just fit your fingers. I loved my flute from the first time I held it. Week by week I met with Mr.

Honey slowly moving up the scale of skill. No melodies yet but my notes were honest and full of promise.

When spring came, I was included with the few who had risen to the top-District Orchestra. Thrilled, I longed to be part of the flute section, filling the air with sweetness. The squeaky clarinets were tuning up as I took my seat. There was another person in charge though, not Mr. Honey, someone else. He was moving through the rows of young musicians. I hardly noticed him until he came to me. He put his hands on my shoulders, then moved them down my arms, so from behind me he had me in a hug. I shuddered. This had happened before. Startled, I turned to look at him, and saw a strange smile, something there I could not name, but it said "Danger." He stared at me as if he had a secret, then left. That's all I recall of that day.

That evening, after dinner, I opened the case where my flute rested. I didn't cry. It wouldn't matter, but I knew what I had to do to protect myself. There would be other days of orchestra. There would be bus trips, performances and maybe one on one instruction that would put me with this man.

Could I tell my mother? What good would it do?

She would say, "He's just being friendly. What's wrong with you?"

For the last time, I picked up the flute.

I took the metal rod that was meant to clean the inside. I attached the cloth. I led it through the hollow chamber. I polished every key. I cleaned the mouthpiece. I tenderly placed my flute in its case, closed and snapped the lid and laid it to rest in the back corner of my closet, closing off a part of my life.

I never did cry, not until I wrote this story. Then I cried, for myself and all the children who trust the wrong people, losing possibilities in measures of their lives.

35. PALEONTOLOGY OR BIOLOGY

The first thing I found of importance, was from an Indiana forest, an arrowhead. I kept looking for more, every chance I had. No more arrowheads, but my collection grew anyway. I added a crawdad claw, skulls from small animals, the leg bone of a cow, an Apache tear, along with a few seashells and pebbles, all arranged carefully on my windowsill, unworried about what the neighbors might think, or anyone else, for that matter.

I left for a week at summer camp. My mother, though, knew nothing of my plans to dig up dinosaurs because when I returned home everything was gone. All I could think is that she was embarrassed by the display, too much death to be seen from the street maybe. All my hopes were gone. This collection had taken years. I felt betrayed. I gave up the idea of wearing khaki and digging for scientific treasures, instead I would be a biologist, trading death for life. Maybe.

For Christmas I asked for and got a microscope. While my cousins were somewhere playing hide and seek, I scanned the wings of flies, examined dust from the floor, and looked hard at the scaly skin from a healed blister. I was within hearing range of my aunts and mother, halfway listening to their diagnoses of their children's failures and successes. I didn't care about what they said about me, but I listened anyway. I was in my own little world, the world of biology, absorbed in smaller things.

For extra credit my sophomore year in high school, I wanted to do a project that would ensure an A, something related to biology. My mother happened to mention a problem with a gopher at the Salt River Project where she worked and that the landscaper had killed one. Hoping it wasn't too late for me to get the corpse and that it would be in one piece, I begged my mother to get the body of the deceased rodent.

I had read up on taxidermy. I was prepared. I took the precious gopher to the storage room, lay it on the worktable, slit it open and removed the guts. I then used boric acid crystals on the inner tissue, got cotton balls from the bathroom, thread from the sewing basket and proceeded to fill the body cavity. As I got to the head, I wondered if it would look better if I stuffed its jaws. His mouth pooched out on both sides. He looked more like a chipmunk so I decided the body stuffing would be enough and stitched him up.

I presented him to my biology teacher on Monday at the first of class expecting him to praise my effort. He had just taken out his grade book to take attendance when I held up my gift.

I had hoped to make it stand up or at least have a gopher-like pose, but unfortunately, he lay on his side like a dead animal, which he was. Mr. Jones took one look and stepped back, raised his eyebrows and asked, "What is this?" I explained that I wanted to earn an A, so I did this project for extra credit. I told him all about my dedicated work. He scratched his head, and took the gopher, setting it up on the shelf behind his desk. He appeared to be standing, his little paws crossed in front of his chest. I took my seat. He took attendance. I got an A.

36. BURIAL RIGHTS

The man was sitting at the kitchen table with my parents, his briefcase on the floor at his side, numerous pamphlets scattered out in front of him. My parents seemed attentive. I skidded to a stop on my way to the refrigerator.

"What's going on?"

My mother looked up at me. "We are investing in funeral plans."

The salesman grinned at me and shuffled his stack of cards.

Incredulous, I forgot all about my snack and retreated to my room. I plopped down on my bed to ponder the situation. Neither of them was sick. They were in no danger of sudden death anytime soon. Neither of them was close to retirement, so why the hurry.

Had they even considered my needs?

Later, I asked my mother about it.

"We don't want to burden you at that time. Many people plan ahead so their families are prepared when it happens."

Well, that seemed considerate.

Maybe they saw it this way, whereas I saw it as abandonment.

I was twelve and they were in their forties. No immediate concern for them. I, however, was concerned. As far as I knew, they had saved no money for my college education, only a few years away. I would have to take care of my own future.

If I ever have one, it will be totally up to me.

I watched out the window as Ron Pratt flicked newspapers from his basket, on the left, on the right as he weaved his bike down our street. I could do that, but I learned girls were not allowed to do that job. Luckily, I had started babysitting, first the five kids next door, Johnny, Kate, Mitchell, Stevie, and the baby. I had been doing this for a year, now understanding that I was on my own.

When I had my first fourteen dollars saved, I walked a mile to the nearest bank and opened a savings account. I didn't buy stuff. I saved it all. I felt responsible and hopeful for the first time. Besides continual babysitting almost every weekend during high school, I sorted letters at the post office at night one summer. The next year and the following I worked for the Head Start program as a teacher's assistant having a great time with the four-year-old children of migrant workers. My senior year I ironed the shirts of an elementary school principal every Saturday morning. I saved every bit of it. Good for me. I had disciplined myself. My parents had the right to plan for their demise. I, hopefully, would have enough time and endurance to plan for my life.

37. PUBLIC SPEAKING

One promising Saturday morning my mother invited me to go downtown with her. *Probably a surprise shopping trip*, I thought. *I could use some new clothes.*

Why ask, this was the usual plan, but we didn't end up at a department store. She drove into a parking lot next to a low gray brick building.

"See that door?"

"Yes?"

Calmly she explained, "You are going to take a speech class."

The determination in her voice and her tight jaw told me she meant it, but it didn't mean I couldn't fight it.

Incredulous, I asked "What for?"

But I knew the reason already. I had become increasingly shy to the point where I avoided answering the phone, my voice trying to hide in my throat.

What do I say after I say "Hello?"

Now she had enrolled me in a class to cure me, I guess.

Behind clinched teeth, she said, "Now, get out!"

Reluctantly, and as slowly as possible, I reached for the door handle.

"NOW!"

I opened the door and got out. Immediately she reached over and pushed down the button. I started crying and begin pounding on the glass.

"You can't leave me here! I'm a child!"

This seemed to be a ludicrous statement and embarrassed, I stopped the hysterics. I was twelve. *I never was a child*, I thought.

I had always taken care of myself. I stepped back as she pulled the car forward and watched her drive away. Sniffling and struggling to see, I stood there. I waited, certain that she would drive around the block to make sure I was okay. But no. Minutes passed while I stood there alone. She had left me in a parking lot in downtown Phoenix.

Something could happen to me, and she didn't even care!

After waiting for her return without success, I gave in and went into the building. I sat in the first chair I could find, right by the door. Holding back my tears, I looked up.

To my left sat several rows of adults, no other kids, not even a teenager. People turned to look at me and smiled.

I'm worse off than they are, I thought.

Maybe their sympathy for me made them feel better. All these people are scared, just like me, trying to sail through life without wind in their sails, voiceless in the ocean of words.

But they were adults; They chose to be there. Me, I was tossed off the raft left alone to drown.

One kind woman came and sat by me, offering me a donut.

"Why are you here," she asked.

In between bites, and new-found sobs, I replied, "Because… my mother made me."

I heard sympathetic sighs float across the room. My misery was plain to all.

The following Saturday I had to stand at the front of the room on a raised podium to give the speech I had written. I do not recall one word of whatever wisdom I chose to inflict on these poor listeners. I do remember trying to halt the shaking of the podium with my grip while noticing the quiver in my voice which I could not control. I didn't look up once, concentrating on focusing on the words in front of me.

I finished, wadded up the speech into a ball and returned to my seat, watching my feet as they made their way to my chair.

Every Saturday for several weeks I got in front of these people whose names I never knew, trembling souls who shared the same fear achieved something together. The smiles and applause following each speech, elevated us. We were experiencing the power of the spoken word.

I learned to look at the faces in the first row, then to cast my gaze across the entire room, and eventually to project my voice to the back row. That was enough. Only silent resentment in the car, coming and going. Knowing me, how else could she have done this. She had to be cruel to be kind.

I should have thanked her at some point in my life, but I never did. I could have said, "Thank you for giving me my voice, for the confidence I gained, for the courage I recovered, and for abandoning me at the entrance to the doorway I needed for the life ahead of me, for a future I otherwise, would not have had.

Thank you, Mom.

38. COOKING CLASS

"You are enrolled in a cooking class this summer," my mother announced, as she set the table. This was different than the speech class she had required of me, no shocking surprise yet. I was excited to get to do something new.

The classes were half day. We learned the rules: turn handles toward the stove, but not over the heat; match pan size to burner; use hot pan holders and never leave the kitchen with food on the stove. The focus was on meal preparation. We cooked and then got to eat our product.

It was fun, but there was a catch which I discovered when the class ended.

"See the hands on the clock?" my mother asked.

"Yes," I replied, feeling suspicious.

What was her purpose in this?

Skipping fourth grade not only meant missing the timetables, but it also left me totally incoherent on time, until my mother explained it this way: "The long hand tells the minutes, and the short hand tells the hour."

Up until that moment, I hadn't really cared. The system; bells, or people, parents, told you when it was time to get up, eat or leave, and any other obligations.

So why the sudden urgency?

Continuing in this timely education she explained, "See, the short hand is on the four and the long hand is on the twelve. It is now four o'clock, time to start dinner."

And wiping her hands on her apron, she then reached around to untie the straps in back, took it off and tied it around *my* waist.

"It will be your job now. Pay attention to the time and be sure to start cooking at four o'clock."

Stunned, I had to consider why this was happening. My wonderful summer cooking class had a purpose that I was unaware of until that moment at four o'clock when time took on meaning and I was given complete responsibility for all the weekday evening meals. And just like that I had the power of the kitchen.

My mother for the first time was going to work.

39. ANALYZE THIS

Passing through the house after a morning outside, I saw a book on the small table in our living room, "Handwriting Analysis" by J. M. Bunker, the title in script. The discovery stayed with me for good reason. My mother had bought the course.

In my own little world, arranged around school, meals and bedtime, I never saw her study or even pick up the book, but a couple years later after a move from Indianapolis to Phoenix, she became a Certified Graphoanalyst and started teaching a night class at the YMCA. Later that year, she was a featured speaker on a local radio station, analyzing the handwriting of people willing to be exposed publicly. I was impressed and now saw my mother differently.

"It has to be script," she told me, "Because printing doesn't reveal character." She explained that much can be learned about a person by studying the slant of the writing and the form of the letters. I soon became an unwitting volunteer for her to examine.

"Look at this 't' she said, pointing to my short, fat letter, crossed near the middle looking like a teepee with the flap open.

She showed me a chart to confirm the truth. "A wide open 't' like yours shows that you are stubborn."

Didn't I know that already?

She proceeded to explain that "a "t" should be tall to show independence and strength. She went on, "and the slant should go to the right to show confidence." Next, she advised me, "Cross your 't's" near the top. That shows an idealistic person."

"Now practice!" and she left me on my own to become less stubborn, more confident and idealistic. Her sly manipulation worked because I did as she asked, without an argument. Now that I was convinced, I wanted to carry it further. When our fifth-grade class did book reports, I had access to writing samples. As each student let the now graded assignment float into the waste can, I casually scooped it up as soon as that student's back was turned and slid it gently into my notebook.

That afternoon I brought them out. "What can you tell me about her?" I asked my mother. I only had girls' writing. I didn't want a boyfriend, but I didn't want my feelings hurt by anyone and thought this process would eliminate the problem.

One by one, she examined the script. "Do you see this?" pointing to handwriting that leaned backward to the point of lying down.

"This girl is egotistical."

"What does that mean?"

"It means she's in love with herself.

"Oh!" I could see that. She was a kind of stuck-up kid.

She picked up another one. She took a long look. "The slant of a person's writing says a lot. See, it slants forward, but the letters look like they're falling. This child is depressed."

I'm sure, I thought. She's definitely not fun to be around.

One more. "Uh, uh," she says. "See the letter 't'? Some of them are crossed, but not all of them. This girl is careless, or absent-minded."

"Yep!" I agreed. "She can never remember to turn in her homework."

That was it. I was through trying to find a friend with the detective method, but maybe I could someday get a job with the FBI.

As for my mother, sadly, her career was short-lived because we had bought a house, and she needed to go to work full-time. However, before it was over, she did a courageous presentation for the listeners on the radio when she shared her analysis of Winnie Ruth Judd's handwriting, the infamous woman trunk murderer, part of a love triangle that went bad. A dynamic ending!

Showing me, if you must leave, give them with something to remember about you, something they will never forget!"

40. ROUSING GRANDPA OR RAISING THE DEAD

My aunts and uncles gathered around my mother's dining table, solid mahogany, six brass legs with a leaf inserted. Her two sisters, herself, two brothers and I made six. I was included, at age twelve, the only kid allowed. They needed to surround the table, all hands on the surface to form a complete circle to do it. Whose idea this was I don't recall, but I thought the whole thing was nuts. They loathed their father when he was alive. He was a vicious man who beat their mother and let them go hungry.

Was this a game to them? They were rid of him. Why would they want to bring him back now and what would they ask him? How are things down there, Dad?

The whole thing made me angry. Inside I was boiling.

Dangerous, I thought. *What if it works? Then what? Fire, flames, crashing glass?* But it was decided, so they dimmed the lights and sat around the table with hands laid flat on the surface. With eyes closed, they started chanting," Cliff, Cliff," calling his name. They waited and did it again, in unison.

I may have been there, hands on the table, but I wasn't about to call up Grandpa. I wasn't scared, just angry, filling up my insides with a raging inferno.

How stupid they were! Starting low in my stomach, rising through my chest, I held sway over an intense sensation. I let it build and build. It took a little time. It filled my shoulders, then my arms. I worked it. I fueled it. Finally, when their voices rose, louder and higher, I used it. Under my hands, the table rose…and fell. It went up fast and down faster, with a thundering, frightening slam.

Had they forgotten? He was just as terrifying dead as he was when alive. The séance ended. No one spoke. They kept their eyes lowered and got up from the table. I sat there for a moment watching them go, wondering… *Whose side am I on?*

41. A SNAKE AT THE DOOR

Lots was going on behind the scene at church. It seemed some people were unhappy with the preacher. Pockets of supporters formed as did other folks who wanted to dismiss him. My mother didn't discuss it, but she posted a scripture verse on the refrigerator about "whitened sepulchers" and I took it to mean she was displeased with all the gossip and division in the congregation. It got so bad that one Sunday the poor man broke down and sobbed from the pulpit. Actual tears ran down his face. The suspense was agonizing.

About this time, my piano teacher, who was also the choir director, whacked my hand with a ruler when I hit a sour note. It didn't hurt my hand, but it caused my sense of indignity to surface. I told my dad, and he chastised her for it. She punished him by kicking him out of the choir. Sadly, the one thing he loved was to sing, especially solos such as, "How Great Thou Art." No more solos. No more lessons for me. All are punished. Very Biblical. Everyone wanted vengeance.

During this era, I had the chance to be a junior camp counselor, which meant that I didn't have to really do anything except hang around the kids, enjoying a nice cool vacation in the mountains. The week was going well, and the food was ok. Just before dinner one afternoon, I was asked to get the girls out of the showers. The girl's lavatory was on a hill above the main campground. I ran up the hill and circled around to the door. I could hear the water running and the laughter of the girls who were having a great time splashing each other, but I stopped abruptly when I got to the building. There, on the step, exactly where sandaled feet would soon stand, coiled a rattlesnake. I was well out of striking range but that didn't keep my heart from pounding.

"Hey!" I yelled. They didn't hear me. I yelled again. "Hey! Don't come out yet! There's a rattlesnake on the step!" They heard me that time. Screams and crying.

"I'll be back," I told them. "I'll get someone."

I ran down the hill faster than I had on the way up. At the canteen, I slammed open the screen door and called, "Anyone here? I need help!" Shortly, the minister in charge appeared.

"Okay. What is the emergency?" He seemed annoyed.

"There's a rattlesnake on the step outside the girl's shower." I spit it out, gasping for breath. "So, the girls can't leave."

He gathered four men and headed up the hill. The snake was still there. I had hoped it would be gone, but then maybe I would be the one who, "cried wolf." But no. Here was the proof.

At the sight of such a crowd, the snake raised his head and swirled, his head and eyes locked onto the movement of the men who were forming a semi-circle in front of the building. The snake advanced. The men stepped back, surprised at the bold move. They bent to pick up stones. The larger, the better. The snake was trapped, and it began to dart and slither. Unable to figure out which direction it would take, the men pummeled it with stones. Some hit the target, others missed. Again, they gathered stones. The snake had sustained an injury, but dramatically rose higher with dignity and began rattling its tail in warning. That didn't matter.

If they all just stepped aside, it might retreat to the woods from which it came. But the stones came again. The men were now jeering and laughing. *From nervousness?* I couldn't be sure. Stone after stone flew. The rattler writhed, tying itself into a continuous moving knot. The men came closer now. The stones few harder and faster. At last, its knotted self lay still. Its head broken, almost off. The rattle still shaking. The laughing continued.

I had seen enough and turned to leave. I don't know what they did with the dead snake. I didn't care. It was brutal. I wanted to cry. For the snake. How cruel it all seemed!

Was there any other way but stoning it? How appropriate for these men to turn to ancient Biblical methods to rid themselves of danger. I was disgusted.

Back home, I announced to my mother that I was leaving the church. The pettiness, the arguments and now the cruelty, all gathered into a hard knot in my stomach. There were no heroes here. No saints. No holy temple. It ended for me.

After missing a few Sundays, my mother asked," Would you like to attend a different church?"

Looking up from my reading, I replied, "Okay."

I chose the red brick one across from the park where I got a drink of water from the fountain at before I began my long walk home from the library.

"I'll take you," she said.

And so, I began my search.

42. CAT TALES

Creamy-colored, fluffy, full of fur, a cat that filled my arms arrived near my front door when I was seven. I believed that he or she had come to be my very own, so I gave it a name. This was my first cat experience and so I had my father get the camera to document my acquisition.

That night at dinner my mother asked what I would name the cat.

"Cracker," I replied. "after my favorite snack, saltines with butter."

My words hit my father like a bursting party balloon, slapping a napkin over his mouth to catch the food he was choking on due to my remark. Once again, my lack of vocabulary had made me feel stupid. *How did I know that "cracker" was a word used to describe a poor, white person from the south?* I had little experience with words and even less with cats as Cracker left never to be seen again.

A year later we moved to Arizona, but our furniture never made it. While our parents looked for a dresser, my sister and I played with three kittens who were nesting in the back of the store.

My parents bought furniture and the store owner generously blessed us with the three kittens which we named Tabby, Bright Eyes and Sugar. Sugar sat on my lap as I practiced the piano, and above my shoulders when I watched TV.

Unfortunately, my father's prejudice would cause her death. *How do I know this?* Behind us lived a Mexican family and one of the boys would cut through our yard in the morning on the way to school. He never asked. He just did it. It was much further if he left his street, took a long block south, then east three houses, with four more to pass to get where he would be if he came through our yard. I know it angered my father and I am certain he said something to the kid. I can only guess what words he said, but I heard him mutter, "Mexicans" under his breath so, I figured he called him names.

We got back from my aunt's house just after dark after celebrating Christmas and as always, I went to find Sugar, but my mother blocked the back door.

"You can't go out there!"

I knew right then she was dead, but how? And why couldn't I see her to say goodbye?

They said a bike fell on her, but I didn't believe that. My mother's face showed me what I could not see for myself, and my father rapidly shoveling a hole in our backyard in the dark told me everything I could only imagine. The kid quit coming through our yard and Sugar was dead. Add that up.

The next day, with tears dried in our eyes, my sister and I made a pact: to save our money for a statue of St. Francis, in memory of Sugar. The fund hadn't even been counted when Claire kicked her shoes off in the living room where one landed on the piano keys breaking one of the interior strings. Supposedly to pay for the repair, my mother took our pitiful savings. We never tried again for that statue. I figured my father didn't want any Mexicans in our yard, and my mom sure didn't want any saints.

The other two cats lived for many years and were inseparable. The following year, my freshman year in high school, I went to Carl Hayden High, which was placed on double session due to high enrollment. I started in the late morning and arrived home by bus around five. Every day, there they were though, my two cats waiting for me at the bus stop a block from my door.

"Isn't it weird?" the kids said. "How those two cats are there every day?"

"Yeah," I would say, "weird," as I got off the bus, waiting until it was gone to go home with my two cats following me. They knew I would protect them.

43. PROMISES AND PREMONITIONS

The west side of Phoenix disturbed me. I didn't fit, but I didn't realize how narrow that world was until I saw the sights in Scottsdale where my uncle had an insurance agency near Main Street on Scottsdale Road. Scottsdale had class. Art was important there. No such thing on my side of town. The art I enjoyed came to me because our class took an art test. Whatever it assessed I was the only one to pass it and was bused once a week to another school where I got to draw.

One evening I was exceedingly angry with my whole existence-my family, school, lack of friends, just everything. I walked to the edge of the driveway thinking I would just leave, go somewhere, but where? It was dusk, just after dinner. To the east, I could see the glow of red on the famous landmark atop Camelback Mountain, the Praying Monk, kneeling, head bowed facing north. I stared at this figure and swore to the setting sun with all my might and every ounce of strength within me that the day would come when I would see his silhouette against the western sky. Deep in my heart I made a promise, that it would happen...someday. I was ten.

Two years later at the Phoenix Zoo, I was standing on the bridge outside the red schoolhouse watching the water flow beneath my feet as laughing children ran past me. I wanted the feeling of contentment that I felt at that moment to last. There, I made myself another promise. I would, at some point in my life, work here.

On the way home from one of our visits to Scottsdale, we stopped to get gas at a station on the corner of Camelback and Scottsdale Road. I went to use the restroom, and as I washed my hands, I glanced out the window. What was there to see but an empty lot behind the station and the side of an ordinary shop, just a beige brick wall. I turned and looked. I stared. This place meant something, but what. I had never been here before. A weird feeling came over me. It was unsettling. This place, without identification or signage of any sort, would be significant in my life. I don't know how I knew or why I was told years and years before it happened, but I knew through and through that it would be important someday. I was held for some moments in wonder as I considered.

What could this possibly mean?

I do not believe in fate. I do not believe in destiny. I do believe in myself, but mostly I believe in divine intervention. Years passed. Promises are stored like mementos from state fairs, but they resurface when events reopen the memories.

My husband decided to buy a business. After searching through multiple opportunities, together we chose a bicycle shop. The location-Camelback and Scottsdale Road. The building was the one I had seen from the window of the service station when I was just a kid. This was meant to be, foreseen and predicted.

For three years I sold bikes, often Bianchi's to wealthy triathletes, mostly attorneys. I really loved Bicycle Works, but the shop was too demanding, and the marriage was winding down to a dribble, as was my endurance. It didn't last.

I had made it to the other side of Camelback Mountain, and the monk was still kneeling, facing north, leaning into the sunset, and I was still standing.

As for the zoo, I worked there years after the divorce. The pay was low, no insurance, but I kept my promise. For two summers and into the fall, I wore the khaki uniform. Ideally suited for my artistic side, the job required the creation of cardboard animals to be used as behavioral enrichment for the lion and tiger. Only wheat paste could be used on the form of the soon to be victim for the big cats, that and tempera paint. On Monday, I cut out cardboard, slicing it so I could jam the pieces together into a shape resembling prey. The kids decided on a penguin first. It wobbled a little, but still at three feet, its height could entice an attack. On Tuesday we painted furiously since our creation would be center stage on Wednesday morning when the keeper, after placing a hunk of meat into the body of our penguin would offer it to one of the big cats. The penguin stood, with its huge, frightened eyes, in the enclosure as the tiger stealthily approached. Hopefully, the cat would display its prowess as a huntress. Lots of suspense created from simple supplies, kids and imagination.

    I went on to Harmony Farm, a part of the zoo with domestic animals. At the schoolhouse I tended the worm bed, handed out wool bits from freshly sheared sheep, managed to feed the goats, held Guinea pigs and rabbits, and fed the chickens. I drove a golf cart furiously on the back roads of the zoo, and helped kids get onto mules. Nothing can compare with the fun of this job, except that of teaching high school English, which I was also destined to do.

44. NOVEMBER 22, 1963

Some say history is made, but I think history is lost, all the possibilities of a precious chance for the best to happen. This was the last day of normalcy in America. Of course, nothing was ever actually *normal*, but the sun did come up, and stars were seen at night, and everyone was safe in "The White House," we hoped.

That was my junior year. In American History I asked questions, not realizing my thoughts, put into pointed inquiries, provoked discussions. My teacher gave me the greatest compliment of my life, enjoying the shared dialogue more than the dry textbook. He called me a Catalyst. Basically, it meant by adding my input to the mix, there would be something new, maybe an explosion. Anyway, I was honored.

Mr. Cognac was my favorite teacher, even though history wasn't my favorite subject, English was, but I wasn't fond of American literature, except for the Transcendentalists, who, like me believed every rock and flower was sacred. At least, that's what I took from it.

I had already researched the Atomic Bomb, but I read *"Hiroshima"* anyway. Years later protesting on the anniversary of the bombing, I chalked the shadows of bodies around the capitol building at three in the morning with other opponents of nuclear proliferation, commemorating those who instantly vanished with the flash.

I got into orchestra, despite my incompetent piano playing.

"Yes, I play the piano," *but not well.*

Enthusiasm has nothing to do with timing and accuracy. Luckily, Mr. Lucky, I shall call him, had need for a percussionist, someone who could read music, count measures, hit a gong, ring a triangle and was able to sit and wait to do something. I could do that for an A.

The baton in Mr. Lucky's hand was striking up the orchestra with the first few strands of *"Beethoven's Fifth Symphony,"* when the voice of our principal broke in, the chords of sound breaking and falling around us with the news that President Kennedy had been shot in Dallas, Texas. Shocked into silence, we waited to be dismissed to our last class, but a second message overhead gave us even worse news.

In history class, Mr. Cognac was sobbing uncontrollably, his head cradled in his arms on his desk. With a motion, he dismissed us early, never looking up.

I sat in front of the school waiting for my father, my ride home that day. The November sky hadn't changed. The leafless trees still stood tall. We realized though, the world itself was lost and none of us knew where we would go from here.

45. THE RAT STUDY

The following year, after my gopher project, I took chemistry. I wanted an A in this class too. There was so much to memorize, and my partner was a jock who needed my help to pass a class I was struggling with myself.

"What can I do to earn extra credit?" I asked Mr. Conrad, who always looked official in his white lab coat.

"Well," he said, "Let me think about it."

The following week he asked me to stay after class for a moment and he described the project to me.

"You will have two rats for the study. For a month you will feed them every day. At the end of the month, you will inject each one with radioactive isotopes, euthanize them, remove their organs and measure the amount of radioactivity in their hearts, lungs, kidneys and liver. To do this project you will need to learn to use a Geiger counter," and he handed me one with a short demonstration on how it worked.

"Are you interested?"

Without giving it much thought, I agreed. I met the rats the next afternoon. Their cage was in a small room at the back of the chemistry class. The food was there, no problem, easy to do.

I didn't name them. I didn't hold them either. They were not pets. I knew I would have to be detached emotionally, and it might be difficult for me. Their days were numbered.

Every day, I checked on the rats, feeding them and giving them water. As the end of the month creeped closer, I began to prepare for the inevitable. I had a syringe and practiced by inoculating an orange from one of the trees in our backyard which at one time had been part of a citrus orchard. I filled the syringe with water, inserted the needle and pushed. I did it again, and again. I did it until juice streamed out onto my shoes. I did this every day after school and after dinner every night, but I knew after practicing long enough that it was useless.

I could not kill the rats. I may have been able to stuff a gopher, but I didn't kill it. It had been dead. No, I could not hurt an animal. Lesson learned.

Immediately, unexplainably I completely forgot about the rat study… the entire thing. I even forgot to tell Mr. Conrad about it, that I couldn't do it. I wiped out my mind without one remaining thought.

Nothing. I never went back to check on the rats. *What rats? What project?* It was as if it never happened, swiped clear of my memory. I did get some funny looks from him though, but I couldn't imagine why, and Mr. Conrad never asked. My grade on the final exam was a D- and my final grade for the semester was a C. I had essentially killed the extra credit, but I escaped killing the rats.

One clear spring morning during my junior year in college, I was returning to the dorm when it hit me. I stopped suddenly. I remembered that I had forgotten to take care of the rats four years ago, how the whole thing had just disappeared.

At the time, I was in the middle of another rat study for a nutrition class. I had a partner, and we did the whole project together. The realization that I had dropped the earlier study with no memory of it made me question my own mind. *Why had that happened?* All I knew was that I could not hurt an animal.

I wasn't worried about this rat we named Speedy Gonzales, though he never got to run, even on a wheel. We just had to feed him a high protein diet and keep track of his weight, fur, attitude, etc. He wasn't going to die. We held him, thinking how cute it was the way he wrapped his long tail around our wrists.

On the last day of class, our professor, her gray hair tied back in a bun, strode into the room, depositing a large glass jar on the lab table with a thud. The sudden noise startled us. She left for a moment and returned with a cage holding the rats. Since they all looked very much alike, I couldn't be sure if Speedy was one of them.

On the counter she had placed a box of cotton balls and a jar of liquid.

"Today the rats will be euthanized," she announced coldly.

I raised my hand hesitantly, while hoping other students would join my protest.

"But why? Can't they be given away as pets? Why do you have to kill them?"

"No," she said coldly, "There are legalities involved. They have served their purpose."

Then, she unscrewed the lid and with her white gloved hand took one rat by the neck and ceremoniously dropped it into the jar. I couldn't watch.

"What was their purpose?" I asked, disturbed.

Was I the only one with any courage?

In a startling statement that seemed unrelated and ridiculous, she proclaimed, "Now you will always remember to eat breakfast."

I eat breakfast because I'm hungry, not because of guilt over the lives of rats.

She was insane, inviting us to an execution.

I stayed until the end of class although I really wanted to run out the door. I did not watch her drop living rodents into the jar. I did not watch the struggle. There was no sound. The class was silent. When it ended, I rose from my seat, pushed my chair under the table and promised myself that I would never miss breakfast, not ever.

46. MY MESSENGER

I left school one spring afternoon of my senior year and headed home, taking a shortcut across an open dirt lot. Far to my right stood a row of stunted cottonwoods, once a common tree in Arizona. To my left across the empty road were the boring brown tenement apartments where the unfortunate poor made their way through life. Behind me, my high school, emptied of students on this late Friday afternoon. I was despondent. Nothing had been saved for my college education. It had not once been discussed in my house, and I felt hopeless.

I had counted my money, saved from years of babysitting, ironing and other jobs. There was only one more summer ahead of me to earn more if I was going to college. At this point, my plan looked unlikely. My depression deepened. I needed to leave home. I had earned my independence if not in cash, in life experience.

At that moment, I heard a soft sound above me, the light, tender whirr of wings, and I looked up. If I had stretched my hand above my head, I could have touched its face. Wide, oval eyes looked directly into mine. White wings spanned the sky, closing off the sun. Over me, shading me, I felt caressed, and in my head, I heard, *"Everything will be alright. Things will work out for you."*

Astonished by this beauty and the prophecy, I stared into the sky. I looked again and again, turning in all directions, but the owl was gone. *Gone-but where?* No trees-no clouds. The sky was clear. You would think it would be easy to spot a large white owl against a clear blue sky, one with a three-foot wingspan, but try as I might, he had disappeared.

What a huge significance this would have on my life! But did it really happen? The deep despair I had felt went with him. My spirit flew like his with an assurance that I had never felt before because no matter how hard I worked, or how much I saved I never felt secure. Now, for the first time, I did, and it was magical.

That same afternoon I told my mother, for the first time, that I wanted to go to a four-year school. No junior college for me although she suggested it. No, I needed to have the consistency of one place. I used the argument that I had gone to three different high schools and wanted to belong this time to just one place. She heard me, she listened, and she acted.

My mother, who had two years of college herself, went to the high school and met with my counselor, either due to my insistence or the magic of the white owl. Thanks to their efforts on my behalf, I received two scholarships and was able to go to

Northern Arizona University and although I had to work pretty much all the time during those four years, I already knew how to do that.

– Chapter 5 –

47. THE TERRORIST AND THE POLITICIAN

The Terrorist

Surviving college meant working, working at whatever I could find, working full time every summer and part time during the year, anything to move forward because I was my own support.

After working the desk in my dorm my freshman year, I began to reach out for more jobs. Babysitting at church nurseries on Sunday mornings proved to be valuable as the services were timed far enough apart to work for both the Catholics and the Presbyterians.

My junior year I found a job tutoring foreign students in English. After a couple weeks of waiting, I was offered a student from Kuwait, *Said*. He spoke English okay, but he had no concept of sentence structure. Try as I might, my tutoring efforts couldn't supply him with enough language to write adequately. Often, I would fix his work, hand it back to him and try to get him to write a second sentence. It was a continuous struggle in more than one way. The problem I had with *Said* wasn't just his lack of ability; it was his insistence on dating me. I was engaged and explained that to him, but it made no difference. He was determined, but so was I.

That summer was the six-day war in the Middle East, 1967. I had little interest in world events far from me, but he was intensely emotional on the subject, thrilled, gloriously enthused when his side won. It scared me that anyone could be so jubilant over war. I quit tutoring him, as there was no solution to his impossible English or his harassment, but apparently, he was still angry over my rejections.

I hadn't seen him for a while, then out of nowhere he suddenly appeared on the sidewalk at the side of my cousin's car as we passed through the campus. She was taking my cousin Paul and I to lunch. Her backseat was stuffed so full that the two of us had to shove ourselves in closely just to fit. As we passed *Said*, he apparently noticed the close arrangement the two of us had. If anyone had seen the pile of belongings next to us, it would have instantly explained the situation, but he had his own belief. At that moment his eyes changed. The fierceness in them was terrifying. If hatred could be seen, I saw it then. I felt he had the capacity for great violence, a man, who in the right circumstances would be very dangerous, and I felt afraid, glad that I had no more connection to this person. I am certain he eventually acted on his vitriol. No one knew the word terrorist at the time, but most likely, back home in Kuwait, he became one. God, I hope I was wrong.

The Politician

That same year our campus, Northern Arizona University, had a visit from Attorney General Robert F. Kennedy. He was there for the Bureau of Indian Affairs and met with the dignitaries in the gymnasium, but he had one meeting downstairs just under the bookstore.

Earlier, I tried spotting him from the door of the gym, but I wasn't allowed in and couldn't find him in the crowd. When I learned that he was going to be in the bookstore basement, I situated myself on the stairway at the railing with my Instamatic camera, so I could not only see him as he left but also get his photo. It seemed I was the only fan. Students brushed past me going up the stairs, annoyed at having to step around me, but I was not moving.

The door below me clicked open and I heard the mingling of important voices. Suddenly there he was, four feet from me. I snapped a couple pictures. He looked toward me, a least almost, and then he was gone.

We were told that the senator would be making an exit through campus on Saturday morning at 8:00 am. I knew where I would be, and it wasn't in bed.

The next morning, I stood on the sidewalk, fifteen minutes early, just in case and waited. Very soon, in the distance, I saw a convertible slowly coming my way. No one drove that slowly on this street, so I figured it was him. No camera this time, I just wanted to wave to the man, someone who I felt had the integrity our country needed; someone I could trust.

Strangely, no other students were out that morning. It was just me, only me, waiting. He was sitting in the backseat of a convertible, balanced as famous people do, his feet on the seat. He saw me and waved to me. I waved back and kept on waving as he passed. I watched until he was gone.

Two weeks later I was home for the summer watching the Primary Convention in California. I heard the shots. I saw the cameras flailing, then cast down on his expressionless face. The panicked voices, the screams, the confusion, but mostly the inability of those in charge to explain to me and the nation... How? Why? Again? I had watched him pass by me on campus. Then I watched him pass from this life.

I turned off the TV, but I didn't cry. I wanted to, but my heart held too many tears. They might have drowned me, if I had let them flow.

48. LOCKED OUT

The summer of my junior year I lived off campus for the first time, in a house shared by two women professors who took off to Europe. There were four of us with two bedrooms, two twin beds in each. I think it was the first time on our own for everyone, so we had some house rules. We pooled our money weekly for groceries and took turns cooking and cleaning. There was only one house key so the last person leaving the house put the only key we had under the front door mat. Anyone who had a ride to Phoenix left as soon as possible on Friday afternoon. On that Friday I had no plans to leave.

I was riding a bike, loaned to me for the summer by a generous guy I hardly knew, Val. Like Prince Valiant, he was my shining knight. His bike made it so much easier to get around even though I had to wriggle onto the seat to get going and leap off at my destination as the bike was a bit too high for me, and it was a boy's bike. Still, I was grateful.

I jumped off the bike at the front door and threw the mat to one side. For a moment, I was stunned, staring at the bare concrete step where the key should have been. No key! I frantically searched the area around the door, the grass, etc. but there was no key.

They had forgotten about me in their haste to leave town. I sat down on the step, feeling completely lost, watching the final rays of the sun disappear into the night. I felt the first cool breeze of evening, wishing I had taken a sweater with me when the day was bright and sunny. The sounds of traffic and the lights of the city were somehow comforting, but I needed a solution. I was cold, hungry and had no place to sleep. My nonchalant roommates would not return until Sunday night, two whole days from now. Only God could figure this one out, so as usual in such a dilemma, I asked for help, praying for an answer.

It suddenly dawned on me that I did have a place to go, at least a possibility existed. In the dorm where I had spent the first three years of my college life, there was a person on the second floor who had an apartment.

Did I know her? Had we ever met? No and no. What was her name?

I tried to remember. I thought it was Ronnie, or Rhonda, or Rita? Her responsibility was to help with problems that might arise with the residents.

Did I qualify? Maybe. I had been one for three years. Would that count?

There really was only one choice, so off I went on my glorious steed of a bike into the now dark night. As I neared the south end of campus, I remembered her name. It was Ronnie! I knew she was black.

It didn't matter to me. Would it matter to her?

I had never met or ever even spoken to a person of her color. Always curious, when I was six, my mother checked out a library book for me. Full of photos of African Americans, this book intrigued me. There were kids in Halloween costumes, at birthday parties. Pictures showed them playing games together, eating with their families, riding in cars, all going about normal activities of life. This was my only introduction to these people. Now I would have a chance to meet someone of another race. I was both nervous and excited.

I knocked tentatively, hoping she was there. She was and she opened the door.

Did I look needy?

I don't know, but I explained my situation, emphasizing that I had lived in the dorm until recently. Then, I made my outrageous request, "May I sleep on your couch tonight?"

Of course, I needed two nights, but one thing at a time.

She replied with little hesitation, considering she was allowing a total stranger into her home for the night. My relief was genuine, and I thanked her profusely. She also provided a sandwich and a glass of milk, to me, a drowning victim washed up on her shore. I slept, exhausted from a furious bike ride and my heightened anxiety.

The next morning, we talked over breakfast, so I was fed a second time. I learned her parents were both professional people, her father, a university professor, and her mother, a nurse.

Meeting a real person was so much more rewarding that looking at pictures in a book. She was kind to me, generous and open beyond anything I could have anticipated. I thanked her for hospitality and started to leave.

"You can stay tonight," she said, smiling.

Again and again, I told her how much I appreciated her help.

I left to go to the library that Saturday morning, where I spent the day. Where else can you go when you have no money, and your friends have left town, all but one, that is.

49. STINKIN' SWEET REVENGE

No way to bake a birthday cake while living in the dorm. My roommate, Gina, asked me to call her mother while I was home for the weekend and ask her to do it, then deliver it to me to bring back up to campus, "NAU".

On Sunday afternoon her mom came to my front door, thrust the cake at me, glared, and stomped off.

What was that about?

I called, "Thank you," as she drove off in a fit.

Back on campus, when the time came to celebrate and all were ready for cake, Gina lied, saying I had rudely called her mother and asked her to bake the now installed cake with candles already ablaze.

I was stunned! At that moment, hateful looks coming at me and accused wrongly, I retreated without a fight and without a bite of the cake I had delivered. I left that group behind, fairly easily, as they did not know me and were ready to believe a blatant lie without question, but as the year loomed ahead, with no way to change roommates, I suffered silently and just went to class.

I no longer spoke to Gina.

Then I found *my* sweater in *my* closet suffused with Topaz, an Avon product, her usual scent. On a rainy day, my shoes on the closet floor were soaked clear through and I hadn't worn them.

"Leave my stuff alone!" I demanded, turning to look her way, but that didn't end it.

One morning I awoke to a pile of snow at the foot of my bed. She had opened my window that night as I slept, letting the winter in on me.

The misery of living with an enemy was squelching my spirit. However, an unusual idea came to me one rare sunny Sunday afternoon in the northern winter. In biology class, I had been in the process of dissecting a fetal pig. The body cavity was now open, the organs displayed. Taking the pig from storage was easy. The little bundle and I returned to my room where Gina was engrossed in reading a magazine, lying on her stomach, knees bent, waving her feet casually, totally relaxed.

What an opportunity for revenge!

Without speaking I unwrapped the piglet, supported by newspaper and gently slid him onto the magazine, right under her nose where the aroma of formaldehyde would impress her. She screamed, holding her nose, leaping backwards off her bed. I rewrapped my class project and returned him to the lab where we would reunite on Monday.

No other clothes disappeared from my closet. No more snow on my bed.

A year later, during my sophomore year, I got an apology from the birthday girl, who had received the problem cake. Now that she and Gina were roommates, she had learned from her own experience as I had, and apologized to me.

Worth the wait.

That first winter it snowed as always, but so very deep. After class, I struggled through the snow, packed waist deep on both sides, nose numb and red, just wanting to get back to the dorm out of the freezing cold, but just outside the door, two guys I didn't know were playing with snowballs. They were just waiting for a victim, and it was me. Laughing and hollering, one of them shoved a handful of icy wet snow chunks down my back, inside my thick, no longer warm, green corduroy coat. The jerk and his friend were hysterical with success.

I went inside, took off my now wet coat, stomped up to my third-floor room, pulled the window open and yelled.

"Hey! You! Come here!" He recognized me, at once, of course, but he didn't know me. *Not at all!*

"Come closer," I said.

Still grinning, he was right below my window. I let loose with my hardest throw, my best aim, lobbing the largest grapefruit I had from my family's trees right onto the center of his forehead, throwing him into the snow where *he* would now be cold and freezing, smelling the sweet scent of citrus as the grapefruit split in two, juice running down his face. I slammed my window shut. I didn't kill him. I just taught him a lesson.

Just like I did Gina.

50. WAY TOO YOUNG

Skipping the fourth grade made me one of the youngest one in my class forever onward. At seventeen, I left for college. Other students, I later learned, had discussed plans with their parents, such as major, money management, career goals, and so on, but not me. *Why start now?* I had always run my own life. I chose to major in English with an art minor, loving both books and brushes.

Three years later and anxious to start my real life, I signed up for student teaching at my old high school, close to home so I could live there during the weeks it involved. In November, at age twenty, I was married.

In December, I started my career training.

In January I had final exams, followed by early graduation and a move to Virginia. I considered myself ready, ready to conquer the adult world, one month into age twenty-one. Not too much. Not for me. But I was too young to know.

Some of the students in my classes were friends of my sister who had graduated the year before. Discipline? How do I handle that? No one taught that in my education classes. My supervising teacher gave me the entire job after a week or two of advice, and I started teaching.

Did I do it well?

My terror kept me behind the desk where I wrote assignments on the board. At night I graded papers until 11:00, crying, careful not to let my tears fall on their work.

Did I know that I didn't have to assess everything?

I just gave them more and more work.

What did I teach them?

I do not recall, but I ended up never wanting to touch American literature again.

Was I observed during those lessons?

Probably, but I don't remember. I was in a fog, drifting through the required motions to reach the shore where I could just disappear. I felt abandoned to a fate for which I was not prepared. Sure, I knew the material, but those kids scared me.

How could I ever do this again?

I walked home after the students had left, but one day a brave boy whistled at me, a long courageous wolf whistle that hung in the air like mistletoe.

My dignity was threatened. "Is that any way to treat a teacher?

His defense, "Oh! I'm so sorry. I didn't know you were a teacher."

Neither did I.

I sure didn't feel like one. I was too young, way too young.

– Chapter 6 –

51. THE ATTIC DREAM

There is no floor on which to stand in this attic. Iron pipes and wooden boards trace across one another where I place my feet, giving me places to stand and hand holds as I search. I look down and can see that I have climbed quite high but looking up is impossible. I must concentrate to hold on, looking for structure, but it doesn't exist.

I awake confused. What does this dream mean?

The attic was in the house where I lived during the first year of my marriage, only in reality there was no attic, only a second floor which we rented from a kind Armenian woman. No attic, only a bedroom, living room, small kitchen and a bathroom situated around a hallway, an old house with creaky boards and drafty windows, no attic. I needed the dream to learn about that year, but while I was living it I could not examine it, how it altered my life, how I was trapped.

The house was on Forest Avenue, two blocks from the Atlantic Ocean in Norfolk, Virginia, a Navy town where my husband was stationed for his last year of duty. I graduated from college early so I could join him there.

What did I expect from him?

At first, we played cards in the evening. I wanted to walk through the neighborhood together, but he wasn't interested.

During the week I dragged a cart full of dirty clothes to a nearby laundromat. Sometimes I took a cab to the commissary to buy groceries. My husband was on the ship more than he was home, but it made no difference. We were two rafts adrift at sea, only I couldn't look at it.

It would get better, I thought, only it didn't.

Why had I married him? My mother tried to warn me, but I had never listened to her advice. Why start now?

Many weeks passed. I looked for a job, but the possibilities existed only for true Virginians. I was a Yankee, tried and true, wasting time, taking buses to interviews all over the city. Sure, I might have taken a teaching job, but I was terrified, completely incompetent to stand in front of a high school class at age twenty-one. I needed more life experience.

Finally, I lied.

"My husband and I plan to settle here when he restarts civilian life."

That did it.

I got a job shelving books in the Navy Station Library. As a literature major, I loved to read but this library of gray and green inspired lifers, not me. I saw no novels and the non-fiction books related only to Navy history, battles at sea and biographies of captains who ruled the ocean. I could not have been more bored.

Every afternoon I had my time at the main desk checking out books to sailors who asked me to go out with them. I only had to lift my left hand to show them my ring and they shut up. If a group got loud while sharing their girly playing cards, I had to walk out from behind the desk to where they sat to remind them that this was a library.

That summer I began to have serious backaches. I went to the infirmary on the base.

What a shock! The clinic consisted of cubicles in which physicians sat ready to consult with patients lined along a wall on rough wooden benches.

This was a waiting room? Built during the Civil War?

When my turn came, I described the constant pain that only subsided in a warm bath, then came right back.

He looked at my eyes, pulled down the lower lid and said, "There is nothing wrong with you." He wanted me to believe I had nothing to worry about! I felt like I had been blindfolded and made to walk the plank. Drowning!

Now what could I do?

That night, as my husband watched television, my temperature rose to 104 degrees.

I interrupted his viewing,

"I need to go to the hospital." But we didn't have a car.

"Call one of your shipmates," I groaned. "Tell him it's an emergency."

He argued with me but did as I asked. We made it to Portsmouth, the closest Navy hospital. As soon as I entered, the doctor gave me a quick exam and admitted me. I climbed onto a gurney, but when I turned to speak to my husband he was gone. He left without saying one word of comfort or concern. I was so scared I vomited.

I have no idea how long I was there. My headaches were severe. I would buzz for an orderly, but it took so long that I would fall asleep before medication arrived, only to reawaken in pain. When I was finally able to sit up, I just wanted to leave. Whoever they were, doctors or corpsmen, no one figured out what was wrong with me.

"Maybe a virus," they thought. "Not sure."

I do not think they were qualified in any way. I just had to get out of the emptiness of the hospital to go back to the loneliness of the house.

After viewing the pile of laundry, a sink full of dishes and an unmade bed. I recalled what the minister told us during our premarital visit, "According to scripture, women are subservient to their husbands," certainly, the attitude of the church. Sure enough, I was obviously subservient, and I went to work on the mess he left for me, even though I couldn't stand without shaking.

We left Virgina and although I wanted to visit Civil War Battlefields and see southern mansions, my husband was anxious to get back to Arizona, so my wishes were ignored. I was learning slowing, surely and painfully that if I wanted something I would have to do it for myself, as I always had before.

That realization made me stronger. To reassure myself and to be the person I was meant to be, I had to reexamine my belief system.

First, I was not made to be subservient. I had been my own guide and champion my whole life. The religious belief that made women less than men could no longer hold me and I broke free one afternoon when I had an epiphany. I realized I was the only one stapling paper hats together for a woman's luncheon, just me.

What was I doing here?

That's the moment I stapled right through the fingernail on my index finger on my right hand. It sounds like a painful experience, does it not? Yet, there was no blood and remarkably no pain.

This wasn't why I joined this church. I wanted world peace and equality for women. God was sending me a message to be on my way, so I left after having the staple removed by a kind doctor who was paid by the church for such emergencies. I would stay connected to my creator, but without a congregation, their obligations or appraisal.

I tried to find that first house on Google Earth, but it was just a flat gray square. The house couldn't be found. The attic never existed. I had been searching for my footing with no place to stand.

When I recognized who I was and always had been, my steps became assured, and finally standing on solid ground, owning my strengths, I built my own life. The dream that had occurred repeatedly for years ended, as dreams do when no longer needed.

52. ART PRODUCTION PLUS

Our accountant gave us the bad news. We owed the IRS $6000, and we didn't have it as the bike shop hadn't made enough to cover our taxes. Unlike the jewelers next door who had a 300% mark-up, bikes had a profit margin of 33 1/3 percent. Accessories such as cycling attire, bike seats, computers, locks, and baskets gave us more income, but too late to fix this. I would need to take on another job to pay it.

On Sunday afternoon I took the want ads and started searching on the back pages, figuring I wouldn't find anything anyway. To my surprise, I found an appealing offer seemingly designed just for me, one I would enjoy.

An art production firm needed an etcher to head that department. *What had I been doing for three years but that?*

It was my specialty! At Arizona State University I had worked in intaglio, the correct word for the etching processes. It means incised, below the surface. After receiving a grant in printmaking, I became proficient. So, I made the call, got an interview and was hired, just like that! Perfect!

The location in downtown Phoenix had been a high-end car dealership as I remembered, seeing it in passing a long time ago. Now the area was a string of decaying motels and empty buildings: a bar across the street and a strip joint next door were the only two steady businesses nearby.

What had once been a showroom for shiny new vehicles was now an art gallery. Just at the entrance was the secretary's desk. Pass her and you were at the small concrete box rooms where the artists worked their wonders. My space held the etching press, storage slots for the many plates to be printed, ink, and all the tools and supplies needed for me to use as Head Etcher. It was just me, the only etcher, so the title wasn't needed.

Next to me, on one side was the silk screen department, on the other was the monoprint team, spinning out art non-stop. The silk screen artist had a very unforgiving media and in his moments of frustration he would sling razor blades into the drywall behind him yelling obscenities in his rage. As everyone, except for me, had earphones and their own style of music, nobody noticed but me, and soon he would be back at work.

Located just past his workspace was a tray of nitric acid that I used as needed for etching new imagery on zinc plates. This open tray of acid gave off fumes which were supposed to flow out of the building through a vent on the wall behind it, but when anyone walked by, the fog from the acid visibly followed them as they passed and it worried me. Eventually I would arrive at a solution.

In the meantime, through the open window in my area where the framing department spread out, I could hear the constant blast of air from staple guns. The framers built the frames, cut the mats and glass, assembled the finished pieces, then packaged the art up to send to whatever corporate entity or hospital for installation.

In the afternoon, if you used the restroom just off the gallery, you could hear the beat of dance music from the lounge next door where the strippers performed. One dancer tried to convince us that they were artists too.

Why argue over technicalities?

One Monday morning a red handprint appeared on the brick outside our door, a bloody puddle below it, gave evidence to the news we had already heard. A late night and one of the girls was murdered. None of us were ever there after dark and we never talked about it.

We had one rule: Do not give money to beggars. They appeared randomly, mostly when we were eating lunch, as we sat on the tailgate of someone's truck or on a cement curb in the parking lot, no lunchroom for us.

One morning, as I walked toward the building, I saw one of the homeless pawing through our dumpster. All that was in there was broken glass, scrap metal and oily rags. So, I broke the rule and gave him two dollars, all I had that day. Then, just as I was about to punch the time clock, I felt a tap on my shoulder. I turned to see another artist who had seen the whole thing, but I was forgiven.

"That was okay, "he said. "He wasn't begging."

One afternoon, the owner explained to me that although I was printing reproductions and I was not the originator of the work, I still had to sign my name. Artists, with their hearts in their own work, feel disrespected when used in this way. I disagreed but I was quickly informed that he could make anyone into an artist, implying that I could be easily replaced.

It was true in at least one case when an old worn-out fellow broke down in his truck, penniless and hungry landing right in front of the place. He was taken in and offered a job, and although I never saw his art, he was employed somehow. Years later, the man, now much older, was in the hospital dying. He would have died alone, but for one young artist who wore Doc Martens and camouflage. She claimed to be his lover. So, they let her in because she convinced the hospital staff to believe this outrageous lie, which tells you what the world really thinks of artists. Because of her courage and kind heart he didn't die alone.

The cost for us was our souls. Every day, one of the best among us, would cross the street to drink before making more art, until one day he was hit by a car and killed.

There were days when an impish artist, known for his escapades, would vanish, only to be seen high above the framing department, balanced on the rafters. His time out self-imposed.

The art director, who chose the colors the watercolorists used, met and married a doctor.

New artists would join us. Some didn't stay long. There was always another starving artist to take their place, if not starving, then maybe in debt to the IRS.

Eventually, the problem with the acid fumes was resolved unexpectedly. I was in the process of etching two plates designed for a high-end furniture business. The theme was ducks in a pond. The order was for two hundred prints and the image on a zinc plate would wear down before an edition of that size could be printed. I expressed my concern, and although I had informed our boss of the limitations of the media, I was told to continue working on the edition anyway.

The inevitable happened soon enough. The plates broke down, and in a panic, he approached me for a solution.

I had been working with copper plates in my home studio which can be etched with a salt, ferric chloride, corrosive, but not dangerous to breathe. At this point the system changed. The etching department, me, switched substances. The nitric acid tray was replaced, and I felt heroic. If I did anything right, it was this.

53. HE KNOWS

Apparently, all I talked about was God. At least that's what my husband told our marriage counselor, who would only see us separately. It wasn't true. I may have mentioned God on occasion, but I was in no way promoting Him. Yet, I thought about it anyway. I didn't want this to become a source of argument. As it turned out I had no reason to worry.

One Sunday afternoon I headed across town to visit my parents on the west side. A random thought, a soft suggestion, came to me.

Turn left here. Okay. This was a different route than usual, but I would still get there.

See that little strip mall on your right. I did.

There's a small drugstore – go in. I parked and got out, but I didn't need anything, so I decided to get a pack of gum, wondering why I was here.

Just inside the door, there was someone familiar, our counselor, Dr. Do Right. He stared, looking quite confused.

"I just stopped by to say hi and to confirm our appointment tomorrow," I said.

None of this was true as I was also quite surprised to see him, but I went with it.

"How did you know I was here?" he asked. He seemed stunned, as if he were witness to an alien encounter.

"Guided, I guess. God knows where to find us. I'll see you tomorrow." I casually picked up a pack of Juicy Fruit, feeling supremely divine!

On Monday afternoon, I could see that our counselor was both muddled and agitated. The roles reversed, I was in charge of this session. He stretched out on his invisible couch as I prepared myself to listen, thinking,

I should be in his swivel chair.

Hands folded across his chest, he confessed, "I've always wondered about Moby Dick."

He expressed his thoughts on the meaning of life, often referring to theme, avoiding the spiritual reality he had so recently observed.

After thirty minutes, I ended the session.

"Well, time's up."

I thanked him and told him I would not be back.

Needless to say he needed more help than I could give him.

54. SPARKS WILL FLY!

I had never held a gun, and I never wanted to, except for that old Fanner 50. However, I was aware that under the right circumstances, I might be tempted. Murder was a possibility. Knowing my husband's gun was loaded and kept in the nightstand next to the bed was absorbing all my thoughts, so I decided to secure the weapon.

I opened the drawer. There it was. It held a clip of bullets. I took the clip and put the gun back exactly as I had found it, breathing a sigh of relief.

But what to do now? I put the clip in my pocket and went looking for a safe hiding place, safe from me, just in case. What I needed was a place where no one would look, a place difficult to reach, beyond temptation.

In the living room, I stood looking at my piano. My parents bought it for me when I was twelve from an elderly couple at our church then lovingly refinished it together. It was a player piano, but the bellows inside had long ago rotted away. Still, it had a decent sound. I couldn't hide it in the bench, too available. I suddenly realized how heavy the piano was, solid wood, with all the works still inside, ivory keys and brass pedals. It would work as the perfect place to hide a potential weapon. I reached over the family photos on top and gently dropped the clip onto the carpet behind it, feeling a genuine thrill of relief, knowing I would not go to prison for murder!

A couple weeks later, just at dusk, I was sorting through my art in my studio attached to the house. I had to decide what I could take with me. I had years of drawings and prints to go through. As difficult as this was for me, it suddenly got worse when a moving truck backed onto the front lawn, right in front of the studio door. I kept on working, wanting to leave as soon as possible, while trying to ignore the obvious. My husband was moving his girlfriend in as I was moving out.

Although I was aware of the actual horror of the situation, I continued to fasten my mind to salvaging my work, until I heard the sound of a piano. I froze. Then I strode out the door, my teeth clenched.

I yelled, "Don't play my piano!"

A woman appeared inside the dim light of the open van.

"It's not your piano. It's *mine*!"

Obviously, her piano was still to be unloaded.

I quickly turned around and went back in the studio, slamming the door as I entered.

I was frantic!

What would happen to my piano? I had to figure a way to get it out of there.

That Friday night with one phone call, I arranged a sale. My piano teacher lived just one long block from my house and one street north. She agreed to buy my piano for a hundred dollars, exactly what my parents had paid for it long ago.

On Saturday morning, the next day, I had my truck and I had rope. I found a few willing teenage boys who wanted an adventure. They pulled the piano out the living room door, pushed it across the front lawn and tied it to my truck. Of course, with the piano out of the way, I once again saw the clip where I had dropped it. No longer my problem.

I started the truck and watched in the rear-view mirror as I began my piano moving job. The boys worked to keep the piano from shifting too much as I drove slowly down the block. At five miles an hour it still weaved back and forth but stopping meant it could ram into the back of the truck. It was a delicate operation. Still, no early morning traffic. No curious neighbors looking out their windows. A truly miraculous escape!

The teens did see something unusual though. As the piano rolled over the asphalt, the wheels shot off sparks, genuine flying sparks, but thankfully not from gunfire. By the time we delivered it, the wheels were all flattened out. The piano I had loved went on to the home of another music lover and I started over. For me it was Independence Day.

55. FACE OFF

I had no money except for the $25 my husband's attorney advised him to give me each week. My sales ability at the bike shop was unpaid, just part of being a partner in the business and marriage. I went to the bank but was rebuffed by the manager, who was abrupt.

"First come, first served," he proclaimed.

When I protested, he said, "That will be for the courts to figure out" and he turned and walked away, leaving me, a partner without the money that was half mine.

Fortunately, I had a small room in the home of an artist, doing chores and making deliveries to thank her for her help. So, I ate and paid for gas with twenty-five dollars. I did it even though I was always hungry. I sold t-shirts I had printed on my etching press, camels, pandas, even snakes, colorful and intertwined. These enchanted my soon to be ex, and unable to resist an image so near to his heart he bought two slivering snakes.

One afternoon, I went to the house to get something and caught the two of them necking on the living room couch.

Did that sight bother me?

No, I was detached from that, but not from my belongings.

The next time I went, the locks had been changed. All I wanted was out, but this required a process server to hand him the court papers, a summons, giving the date and time he had to appear. However, he evaded service, as it is called, not answering the door when she arrived. The divorce was on hold since he never went to court.

Why? It was to his advantage to delay it as he still had the house and all the assets. I just wanted sweet release.

I hired the process server again and again, as there were only three chances to serve him each time, and then it started over. I did this more often than I can remember. Finally, I started watching the house. I parked the car on a side street where I could see anyone leaving. I planned to follow and call the process server when he arrived at his destination, but I didn't see him leave the house, ever.

Yet, I knew that they both knew I was spying because I got a message. On the brick fence of the house, which was facing my car, the word BITCH! was painted in five-inch-high letters, there for me to see. Having been pushed around for so long this message felt like a well-deserved tribute, a tribute to my persistent, annoying presence. I had managed to irritate him to the point of criminal activity, *his own property-vandalized!*

Finally things moved on. I found out he was taking his girlfriend to dinner at a Mexican food restaurant. To my advantage, it was across the street from a Fry's grocery where I could park and watch through my binoculars. The process server parked near the entrance to the restaurant and waited and watched.

Never able to resist a woman's voice calling his name, he turned when she addressed him.

"You have been served, sir!" she snapped, slapping the papers into his hand.

Yes! I watched the entire drama from across the street, the color draining from his face.

Finally, I was in court, on my own, having fired the attorney who did nothing. I achieved the oddly unusual privilege of speaking directly to the judge on the phone regarding my case. She was annoyed by my husband's behavior and was on my side. I was ready.

"You have been evading service, sir!" she stated bluntly, addressing my husband directly, referring to one time my server followed him as he left the house.

"I wasn't in the car when it turned left on McDonald Drive," giving the judge his ridiculous denial.

Ignoring the lunacy, the judge outsmarted him.

"Andrea, would you like to have your husband handcuffed and escorted to the bailiff?"

I didn't hesitate. "Yes. I would. Thank you."

Knowing that he would be irate after this and would want blood, my blood, I decided to avoid that encounter by going up one floor where I could see the front of the courthouse and watch him leave. Soon he came out, looking left and right for guess who. Then, when he was far enough away, I left. My car was conveniently parked close by. He was still looking when he caught me in his sight, but I was too far away to be killed.

I waved goodbye, got in the car and drove off, vowing to never see him again.

56. CROWN OF THORNS

To become whole, it seems necessary to be broken, or face loss, or know pain, a paradox experienced by the greats who became great after destruction of a part of themselves. Consider Beethoven, Goya- their deafness. For others, sight was lost, Milton. For some, much more, Helen Keller and Stephen Hawking. I cannot compare my suffering to theirs, but for me, the loss of my mind, righted me, turned me around, and gave me a reason to go on.

A friend, apparently psychic, but a fact unknown to me, asked to hold my watch. I took it from my wrist and gave it to her. She folded it into her palm, pressed her fingers around it and closed her eyes. I waited. When she looked up, she had a directness in her gaze that was somewhat foreboding.

"You," she paused," are carrying the weight of the world on your shoulders," and she handed me my watch.

How did she know?

I knew, but had to shoulder on, trying to keep going on sheer determination. The next day I requested tranquilizers from my doctor, took one, only one and looked at myself in the bathroom mirror. My eyes would not focus. I tried. I tried hard to have them work together, but I knew those pills were not the answer. I was doomed.

Besides the marriage, the business, the kids, my parents were struggling with all that comes with aging. Miles from my home, I did my best, checking on them with phone calls and staying for a couple hours on Sundays. It was all I had to offer.

One phone call from my sister was all it took to split the air in two.

"I know you are giving 100%, but I need 10% more. That did it.

I hung up on her. Self-protection, automatic!

I could not take one more step without falling, dangerously close to annihilation. I started bath water as hot as I could stand it and sank into it, hoping to drown myself, but as I lay there, my mind began to leave me, to evaporate. I could not lose myself this way. I grabbed a towel, wrapped it around me, went to the refrigerator, took out two trays of ice, dumped them into the tub and got back in the now freezing water.

Staying conscious was all I needed!

Halfway aware, I dressed and escaped into my studio, locking the door, holding back the panic of disintegration.

I took paper and wrote. All the hates, all the mistakes, all the terrors, the fears, the demands and my abandonment filled the page, maybe not all, but all I could remember right then.

Looking out the window, I imagined wild dogs in the moonlight, red eyed and snarling, heading my way. I ignored the knocking at the door and went to sleep on the floor under my etching press, one thing that was truly mine.

Alone, the next day passed slowly, but I made a plan. My husband had booked a three-day trip on Lake Powell. If I went, I was certain I would find a way to drown myself, so I decided to avoid it by being missing when it was time to leave. I stayed away, long past midnight, driving around until I could be safely alone.

Fortunately, just days before this descent into collapse, an artist I knew recognized my anxiety, and took me to an EA meeting, Emotions Anonymous, a program based on the same twelve steps of Alcoholics Anonymous. The meeting that night was at a nearby Catholic church. I didn't participate then, but now I was ready to admit *I was powerless over my emotions.*

I found all the meetings, locations and times, anywhere in town for the next three days and I went to two, sometimes three a day, churches, even a pool supply, working constantly on the twelve steps, writing on and on without eating or sleeping. Time seemed to expand.

On the last night, the meeting was at 9:00 at North Mountain Park. By then I was exhausted, hardly able to focus, much less drive. *I needed a miracle.*

As I left the house and turned to lock the door, I noticed a cassette tape attached to the mailbox with a rubber band.

What music could this be? Could it help me stay awake?

Metallica! An absolute gift from heaven came to my rescue!

I played it loud. It kept me wide eyed and alert as I drove there. I climbed the mountain path to join the others needing rescuing and played it again all the way home. I reattached it to the mailbox, took my pile of Twelve Step words, found a bucket, filled it with sand, threw it all in, lit a match and watched it burn. Slender smoke drifted upward, tenderly carrying away my sorrows, healing my mind. Restoring my soul.

57. RECOVERY

The night I burned my words in the bucket of sand I was on my way to healing. I was functional, but not yet complete, not quite done, not back to being totally myself. Capable of doing mindless jobs, house and office cleaning, a newspaper route, none of which required thinking. No planning required. I continued to go to Twelve Step meetings, like other people who were expecting miracles sometimes they happened.

I found a meeting in October at a Catholic church. The place was packed from the parking lot where booths were set up, to the lawn with games and food. I had arrived in the midst of a school carnival, never realizing Halloween was coming. Even the hallways were jammed with kids and parents. No sign anywhere indicated a meeting. I was suddenly hit with despair, lost in the crowd, feeling quite helpless, still raw. Then, just as I began to panic, I heard a voice in my head.

Follow that man!

From around the corner, confidently moving through the crowd, he came, moving with purpose and direction. My anxiety evaporated at that moment, and I followed him to a fifth-grade classroom. I had made it! I was there! A miracle unquestionably!

During this short time in my life, a psychic, mysterious energy burned just under my skin. I felt it all the time. I felt on fire, but not in a harmful way. It was just a very deep, strong feeling of spiritual power.

What did it mean?

The last meeting I attended was an AA meeting; they accept emotionally stressed people as well as their own. As it ended, the group moved onto the moonlit lawn outside, forming a circle and saying The Serenity Prayer, "God grant me…"

I held the hands of those on each side of me, strangers I would never meet again. With a sense of finality and all my spirit, I sent my best prayer heavenward, the flame I carried within me, through my hands, to heal if at all possible the damaged lives around me.

"It works if you work it."

At the last mantra spoken, and as hands were dropped, to my right, standing five people away, an old fellow stumbled backward, shaking his hands in front of him as if they were on fire. "Hooo leee Mar ee! Mother of God!

His face beaming, standing taller, new, cleansed, joyous, surrounded by the rest, who with sincere love, gave him hugs, handshakes, and pats on the back, all astonished by the event. I watched and then went home, no longer carrying that odd energy.

I cannot explain it. He was receptive. I had a gift. No more miracles. No more meetings. Done.

I had given it back. "Having had a spiritual awakening…"

– Chapter 7 –

58. THE WARNING, GUIDANCE, AND THE RESCUE

As I drove from the mountains of Flagstaff to the Valley below, I was attentive to my speed, going downhill at seventy-five mph, the speed limit. The pine trees flashed past. Suddenly, I heard a warning voice in my head, "Slow down... Now!"

Immediately, I took my foot off the gas and coasted, decreasing my speed by at least ten miles per hour. I felt the car slow, but I didn't brake, hoping that this would be enough, *but for what?*

The instant the car slowed, a doe leaped across the hood of my car. I still have the vision in my mind as the image froze so I could always remember this miracle. She missed certain death and assuredly so had I.

My passenger, astonished by this mystery, asked, "How did you know to slow down?"

Guidance

In my dream there was a gecko on the ceiling in the living room. Alarmed that it would be a victim of my cat, I needed a plan to save it. I asked for a wastebasket and a broom. I would tap it with the broom, knocking it into the wastebasket. I would then release it outdoors where it would be safe. I pushed the broom up, right below the gecko and gave it a small hit just enough to send him falling, but he missed the safety of the basket and instead landed on my arm. I screamed and the gecko ran off to a likely death by cat. Still, only a dream.

Yet, the very next morning, there was a gecko on the ceiling in the living room, exactly as it had been in my dream. Thinking that the failure of my rescue attempt in my dream was the size of the wastebasket.

It was probably too small, so I asked for a laundry basket, surely large enough to catch a small gecko. Again, I tapped it with the broom, very gently, so I would not knock it from the planned trajectory, but just as in my dream, the gecko landed on my arm. I screamed and it ran off to its fate.

I thought about this odd experience for several days. Surely, there must be a meaning, a message I needed to learn. This was the first of my dreams to ever, literally come true and I wanted to know what it meant. Convinced that God was telling me something, it seemed so simple, even ordinary, but I needed this reminder that I would not forget this message to myself.

I realized after much thought that there will be times when no matter how hard I try to fix things, I will not be able to do so. I will just have to live through it.

Much of what I wanted to control was out of my hands. I needed to accept this. It did me no good to fight my circumstances all the time.

This gave me a much-needed sense of peace.

Rescue

I awoke, yet still dreaming, a sense of alertness, within my sleep. I heard a flapping, the sound wings make when a bird is trapped. I looked up to see a pure white egret, damaged and weak, struggling high against the corner of the room in a useless, frenzied attempt to gain freedom. Confused, not understanding that it was unable to fly here in this space, it terrified me.

I knew who this was, and I leapt from my bed extending my right arm toward the talons, hoping the large bird would grasp my arm and it did. It became calm with my strength and, steadily, the glorious, majestic creature and I, left, both gaining our freedom.

It was me who struggled. The egret was me. It came to me in a terrifying yet glorious dream to give me back my broken spirit, to rescue me and protect me as I went forward with my life.

To make me believe in myself again.

59. SILVER INTO GOLD

I had heard that a beginning writer might be allowed in the door of a magazine as a freelancer with the chance that this "silver" unknown could turn into "gold." Everybody starts somewhere, right?

The magazine *"Today's Arizona Woman"* featured women in business. I wasn't a businesswoman, though I had been half of a bike shop when I was married. The thought of freelancing for this magazine kept a hold on me, as if someone was waiting behind this door to welcome me, as if I couldn't fail. This was a powerful feeling, and so I was compelled to try.

Finally, I made a phone call.

"Yes, we consider using freelancers. Send us a sample of your writing."

So, I sent a couple pages of a fiction piece I had started and waited to hear from the magazine.

Two weeks went by without a response, but I was patient. Who am I to make demands?

I had heard that it takes thirteen repetitions of a name to get recognition, so I called them.

I gave them my name again. That would make two.

An apology, "I am so sorry, we lost your sample. Would you please send it again?"

So, I did. My third chance at name recognition.

It turned out this second sample was also lost, *to my advantage,* as guilt was now involved.

"The editor would like to meet with you. Can you come into our office?"

Of course, I can! I grabbed this real opportunity! In person! With the editor!

Her office was everything one would expect, shelves of books behind her and a green glass desk lamp like those on the tables of eastern university libraries, giving the room a soft warm light.

"Why do you want to write for us?" she asked.

"I want to support women in business," I said. I also told her I previously had shared ownership in a bicycle shop, so I had been a businesswoman.

It turned out I could have an assignment, the topic: Fung Shui. If she chose to publish the story it would print in two months; however, I would not be paid for the first one. Still, if it went to print, I would get a second assignment and for that one, I would be paid.

"Yes. I want to do it," I agreed, and set out to learn something new.

At the community college where I had enrolled in a magazine writing class, the library allowed me to check out every book on Fung Shui. I did my research, then searched the yellow pages (available at the time) which had all kinds of experts on the subject, though them were more like fortune tellers I discovered.

Finally, I found a decorator who was willing to talk to me, one who had her feet firmly on the carpet, as this story had to be about reality. I met her at a nearby restaurant, asked questions and took notes. I began to form in my mind how I would approach this story. It had to fit the style of the magazine and be interesting enough to read all the way through. It was a great topic. I learned how the arrangement of items we choose to live with may soothe or disturb us below our level of consciousness.

I wrote the story. It was published, and I went onto do stories on flooring, lighting and tile. With practice, I became able to collect the information and write the story within a three-hour time frame, making I figured between twenty and twenty-five dollars an hour this way. Soon, I had two and sometimes three stories a month.

After some time, I went to the sports arena and met with a Phoenix Suns player. Another time it was a Phoenix Mercury coach, then a Coyote player from Finland. Gradually, I gained admittance into a world I would never have entered except for this profession.

A couple years into this, the Internet was starting to explode and new opportunities for world-wide connections created avenues for unexpected events. A new procedure for heart surgery using laser was being performed at the heart hospital in Phoenix. For this operation a woman was selected whose heart was so weak it took all her strength to walk from one room of her home to another. I met and interviewed her before her surgery, reluctantly discussing the possibility of her death. I needn't have worried. Her understanding of the chance she was agreeing to take, and her acceptance of the consequences was profound. Rather than live as she had been, she was willing and ready to risk her life, and she had faith that it would work.

Directly above the operating table was a room for observation, a theater, in which a circular window on the floor allowed those of us privileged to be there, to watch as the surgeon, using a laser beam, shot streams of light through the muscles of the heart. There wasn't a sudden change, but as I watched with intensity, the heart, at first ponderous and heavy, began to alter its pace, slowly gaining a steady, lighter beat. I could imagine holding one in my hand, feeling the gradual life-giving power return.

Watching such a miracle, I felt honored. For sure, silver had turned into gold.

60. LOOKING FOR AMERICA

Part-time work was for a while, best for me. These jobs could not overlap, but they could be scheduled perfectly. Every ten years, the U.S. Census hires part-timers. Some people ignore or lose the form required to record our population making a job for me. I passed the test, wore the badge and headed to my assigned area, a wealthy neighborhood on the slopes of Camelback Mountain.

I did have some trepidation, talking to strangers, but I was official, supported by the U.S. government, so why worry. I could just stand at the door as required, ask questions, and fill out the paperwork.

After driving up the slanted road, I arrived at homes perched near the mountain top. I parked and walked to the door of the first house, shaded by an overhang above the tiled entrance. I was about to knock on the partially open door.

Why and what to do now?

"Hello?" I called, announcing, "I am with the U.S. Census. Anyone home?" I waited, concerned.

Soon, a woman emerged, looking to be over seventy years of age. The room was dark.

I stayed near the door, as required.

"Would you help me?" She pleaded softly and passed me a screwdriver.

"*What now?*" I thought.

"My doorknob is falling off and I am not strong enough to fix it. Can you do it?"

"Of course, I can," I replied, now understanding the entire situation.

I took the screwdriver and easily tightened the screws.

I introduced myself again, "I am here to help you complete the census form."

"Okay," she said, taking the screwdriver from my hand and thanking me for the task.

"*Oh well*," I thought.

"I broke the rule of not entering the house, but what else could I do?"

The second house, same street, had a double wide wooden door like you would expect to see on a castle. I lifted the iron knocker and let it fall. Waited, and did it again. A woman's voice, and soon a man's spoke.

"What do you want?"

"I am with the census. I need for you to complete the form."

From behind the door, they answered all the questions. Since they both made salaries of more than $200,000, I knew why they were fearful, but sadly, all that money didn't make them feel safe.

Most of the time, it was simple. An apology for not filling out the census form, followed by a willingness to share the number of people in their home, names and ages. People do like talking about themselves, even like this. It soon became routine.

State my name, announce my purpose, and they respond. By the time I had repeated this for several weeks, my routine had become ritualized.

Why I broke from my usual spiel, I do not know.

It was accidental and entirely unplanned. Maybe I was bored, but I know people weren't listening to me anyway, so I said, without thinking or any hesitation, "My name is Andrea Rogers, and I am with the USSR."

I heard myself say it, but the man I was addressing paid no attention to my actual words, and so I was spared humiliation, possible chastisement, or loss of the job. I was right. No one listens!

On the other side of the mountain, just off Lincoln Drive, and winding through narrow dirt packed lanes I arrived at the residence of an elected official, a well-known individual.

I parked and walked to a patio where the Arizona flag and the red, white and blue waved high above me. Music, jazz by Fats

Waller, which I recognized for some strange reason, came from a room at the far end of the house while I stood waiting.

"Do you know where you are?" a woman asked, taking off her sunglasses and looking up from where she was sunbathing.

"Yes, I do," I answered." I am here for the census."

Rising, and wrapping herself in a robe, she complied.

"I will get someone for you. Please wait at the door."

Soon I was escorted into the office of the gentleman I needed to meet, a famous senator. He was kind, friendly and willing to give me the facts I needed. I was honored in a way as this experience was surely unique. I thanked him and left, thinking to myself smiling,

The hawk meets a dove.

61. DRAWING LESSONS

As I walked across the parking lot of the rehabilitation center, I could see my new student, a large Native American man captured in a machine roped with tubes and propelled by wheels. On his face I read a mix of both apprehension and anger. I was concerned.

Would he accept me as his teacher?

I reached him and was introduced. Now, my student, he looked at me and nodded, giving me the start of a smile, and so we began.

I was told about this job by the gallery director who occasionally sold one of my prints. A man had sustained serious injuries in a rollover on the reservation. That's all I knew, except that he was quadriplegic.

Could I teach him to draw?

I had been teaching drawing to children who didn't believe they could ever learn, but they did and they became young artists.

Was he any different?

The first thing the recreation director did was to make certain Ty's mouth stick would hold a pencil firmly. He trusted me right from the start. I would see him once a week for an hour. In between, he would practice the assignments I gave him.

His first lesson was to draw a vertical line, then a horizontal line through the middle adding two lines in between, like a compass. I thought of it as a symbol of energy, a physical exercise and a drawing skill builder.

A week later he showed me his work, well done. I gave him more to do, to draw boxes, nine of them, just squares, but this meant his lines had to start and end exactly where they were needed. He did that too. The third lesson was on values, from white to black, incrementally increasing in darkness with each one within the nine boxes he already had drawn, a difficult task for any beginning artist, but necessary to create form and distance. He did that too.

I worked with Ty every week for over two years. By that time, he was drawing realistic scenes in colored pencil, selling his art to the hospital staff on a regular basis. The head of the John C. Lincoln facility noticed and commissioned him to do the Christmas card that year.

At one point there was a mystical art experience between us. I decided we would both draw a buffalo. Miles across town, I started drawing the animal one evening. I wanted the animal's head in profile, but the buffalo turned and looked at me. I erased and tried again. The same thing happened. No matter how many times I tried to control him, it was the same. This buffalo held his gaze, his dark eyes profoundly serious. Lots of smears and smudges later, I gave up, unable to figure out the problem.

I took my drawing to show Ty. He had his too. Both drawings were done in pencil, and both of our animals were identical in size. Both faces were looking at us and both of our buffalos had the same intense expression, wise and serene. We simply stared at this magic, amazed. How could it be explained, other than, somehow, mystically our minds had a common bond reaching across space, directing us, although he had to struggle differently. I knew his was the more powerful animal, commanding mine to turn, again and again.

His strength as an artist was proven. He could be his own teacher now.

62. GROUP

Art transforms lives. I knew this, so I asked to have a group to work with as I was already at the center teaching drawing to Ty. Group is the word for a class at the rehabilitation center, and instead of students, I had clients. I received seven young men, all under thirty, all with injuries due to accidents, five from motorcycles, and two from serious falls.

The first lesson was watercolor, just moving the paint from palette to paper. Touch the brush to the water, then the paint and onto the paper.

Do you have a memory?

Does a color remind you of it?

Only one responded, his speech garbled, but I understood one phrase, "They left me…they just left me."

His painting was brown and black. It looked like it could be rocks, and actually it was. He had been a world class climber until one day he slipped. Of course, the others left to get help, but all he knew in his head was abandonment. He was still there in his mind, his eyes red with anger, so he threw the chair next to him, and then he cried. No one was hurt. That was the first day.

Everyone painted, but Curt kept it up with dedication, accumulating a pile of watercolors looking like color studies, no line or defined form, but with meaning to him. His anger dissipated over time, perhaps due to his art. In the spring we had an art show. He came, still in his wheelchair, smiling, next to his work, accepting compliments from guests.

Another client, Ernest, after a few sessions, said he had something he wanted to show me. He left the room to ride the elevator to the third floor to go to his room at the end of the hall. It took time, but finally he reappeared, pushing the wheels on his chair with both hands.

Something was in his lap. He held it up, showing us a glass vase, etched with a delicate image of a rose.

He had done many of these before his injury and asked me, "Do you think I will be able to walk again?"

He needed to stand to do sand blasting work. I did not hesitate to answer as I believed, and still do, that no one knows the potential of another human being.

"Yes," I said, "I believe you will be able to walk again."

More than six months later he walked into the day room, proudly demonstrating his recovery. He was met with applause from the group and a hug from me.

He invited me come to his home and meet his family. While there he showed me his workspace and the equipment he used for the glass etchings he was doing again. I learned he had been a foster child in this family and eventually was adopted. I was humbled to meet such loving people.

Until he returned to see me that day, I had hoped that what I said gave him the determination to try to walk, to not give up. When I saw for myself how he had recovered, I believe it did.

63. THE DOLL, THE FLAG, AND SWEET POTATO PIE

A head injury is physical, but the issues that follow are behavioral. One client, new to the group, brought her doll to class, a talking doll, which wouldn't have been a problem except for *her* behavior. She interrupted me often. Not the woman, the doll.

"Will you be my friend?"

My instinct is to be kind. "Cecelia, please keep your doll quiet while I talk."

"Okay," she would answer, but soon, "I love you." We all stopped and stared at the doll who continued talking, "Do you want to play?"

As a child her own mother dropped her out a window, so what business did I have of taking away her toy? At first, she was on third floor of the center where her anxious outbursts caused a huge commotion. So, she was moved from the third floor to the second and eventually to the ground floor ending the problem. I decided, under the circumstances, I could take turns with a talking doll.

Near to the fourth of July, I found several small American flags and stuck them on the table using clay. Time was something they needed to be part of as their days could just run together, so, I planned to share memories about Independence Day and paint some semblance of the stars and stripes in watercolor.

Freddy, a recent addition to our group patriotically grabbed his flag, held it high and made his own parade around the room, humming *God Bless America*. It was such an enthusiastic, heartfelt addition to our day, I decided we should all try to sing.

"Land that I love. Stand beside her and guide her…" and so on, singing an anthem for independence, something we all wanted.

As fall approached, Thanksgiving dinner was anticipated. Dee, a black woman from the south, told us in scrumptious detail about Sweet Potato Pie, so much better, richer and creamier than pumpkin. She sure wished for a piece of that pie as we all did now.

So, in the next few days I did a little research and before the next class, I found a recipe and although I am not a baker, managed to bake a sweet potato pie to share in group. Dee savored every bite, and we agreed that this pie was much better than pumpkin.

It didn't matter that I had only one psychology class in college and no hospital training. I belonged here, learning compassion in a way I never knew. I became grateful and more aware of the fragility of life, of the trials, of the endurance required, things I would never forget.

64. WAGON WHEELS AND SEASHELLS

After a while at the rehabilitation clinic, the hospital nearby asked me for a session. The fourth floor of the hospital was dedicated to car accident victims and as they regained mobility they needed something to do.

I wondered, Why would they want to draw when they could stay in bed and watch TV? So, I knew I would have to enchant them.

A generous framer gave me scrap mat board and I used it to create a background scene to hold the images made by the patients. I painted a prairie, complete with tumbleweeds, rocks and lots of space left for the Conestoga wagons that would circle the camp.

After distributing paper and pencils, I gave my failsafe instructions: Draw two vertical curved lines facing each other but curving outward. I demonstrated. Connect these lines with a straight line across the top, then one across the bottom. They recognized what they had drawn and added the wheels with spokes and the line for the tongue that would hold the horses. Once we cut these out, they taped them to the prairie around the campfire I had drawn.

As they worked, one man shared that he had been a wagon master prior to the car accident. His story about leading a wagon train like ours, amazed the group and it seemed it had been planned to turn out this way.

Who knew? I sure didn't.

A second miracle that day. A nurse came in to collect a patient, "Where is Mrs. Spencer?"

"She left," I replied.

Startled, the nurse quickly ran from the room, "She can't walk." I guess art can do some amazing things.

I began reaching out to assistant living facilities to do art programs. One time I had scallop shells which just fit into the palm of your hand. A group of twelve all in wheelchairs came that day, an empty beach scene was waiting, the ocean waves surging. Everyone had a shell to hold.

"Look at it. Feel it," I told them.

Then I placed my shell face down on my paper and traced it, showing them how to do it.

"Easy, right?"

They all nodded in agreement.

"Okay," I said, "you can start," but none of them were drawing.

I turned to the gentleman on my right, "Are you ready? Any questions?"

"I think I'll just watch," he said in a very small voice, looking down at his lap.

I turned to the next person, "And you?"

"I want to watch too."

Total silence. They were all watching me, so I went around to every one of them and asked the same question. All of them just wanted to watch. I paused for a moment and then I asked the group, "So, what are all of you going to watch?"

That did it. Slowly, but surely, they all picked up their seashells, placed them on the paper and traced the shells. Then I asked them to look at them again.

"Do you see the ridges?"

They all nodded.

"Now draw these lines on the shell you traced."

They did it!

Now they got to watch me. I cut out all their shells, placed them on the beach scene and signed each person's name. The Activity Director displayed the project for a month outside the dining hall. I let them keep their shells, souvenirs of a day at the beach.

– Chapter 8 –

65. CONTEMPORARY TEMPORARY

Private school provided day care for my three-year-old daughter, a plus for the job. I would teach sixth grade English and do an all-school art program for each class on different days of the week, but I got my own education.

Upon entering my classroom one morning, there was a well-dressed man sitting in *my* chair behind *my* desk. I stood in the doorway, unsure of the situation. He lifted his feet from off the desk, slowly, as if he had all day to do it. He then explained his concern about his son's failing grade in my English class, in the same breath offering me a case of Scotch in exchange for an A so he could get the boy into Brophy, a highly recognized Catholic high school. He didn't know I don't drink, and I am not the kind of person to take a bribe of any kind.

"No thanks," I said, approaching my desk expecting to trade places at once.

"He can see me about make-up work. We can start there," firmly placing my briefcase on *my* desk essentially evicting him.

His son never came, so nothing changed.

The school didn't have a library and I required a research paper which needed parent involvement and trips to the public library, but they wrote their reports. In addition, book reports were monthly. Parents, in high demand professionally with little time for errands had this to do also.

One student, Kevin, didn't have his assignment when it was due, telling me, "My maid threw it out." Adding, "Doesn't your maid ever throw your stuff away?"

I looked him right in the eye and said with a smile, "You are looking at my maid."

After that, he had his assignments in on time.

It was different here. I never knew where my job started or ended. An intercom message interrupted my class, "Ms. Rogers, there is a dog on the playground."

"So?" I asked.

"I need for you to get it off the playground."

Surprised by this, "I am in class. I have students."

I had no intention of doing the job of animal control. I had enough with student control.

But other offers arose, "You are needed to clean off the lunch tables for the kindergarten class," and "You will need to go buy art supplies for the classes. You will be reimbursed."

Finally, wondering what else I might be expected to do, I called the Arizona Education Association.

"You are a private school employee and have no rights as such. You may as well be a waitress," I was told.

I got called to the office. What could I possibly have done?

My daughter sat kicking her little three-year-old feet, unaware that she was in trouble, just looking at the photos of the owners and founders of the institution, generations past, proudly displayed on the wall.

I figured it out immediately. A kid had been pushing her around every day. I had asked her teacher to intervene, to prevent this, but she didn't do anything I guess, so my child did it herself. She leaped on him with all her might and bit him. Secretly proud of ability to defend herself, I thought about it.

Was I in trouble?

Really, does a three-year-old grasp the significance of being sent to the office?

A few years later, I was hired at a charter school specializing in the arts. Students had to apply with a portfolio or evidence of talent. Teachers had to be working artists, or writers. I stood at the desk waiting for an application. It happened that the young sculptor I had worked with at another school the previous year was right there at that moment. I was happy to see him and even happier when he recommended me, having been on staff. I was hired immediately!.

Here I would teach drawing and a course called *Contemporary Humanities* which really was a social studies class. I didn't have a degree in that subject, so the curriculum was entirely up to me. Thirteen students were in that class and six young artists in the other. Classes were two hours long, not a problem for the drawing class. They could draw all day without stopping.

The class included color theory, the principles and elements of art and daily timed exercises in each area. Once I took a paper airplane on a string and swung it in wide circles to attempt a motion study. This is no different than a long-ago art teacher who dropped chickens from a roof and had his students draw them descending. Artists will do crazy things for art.

My classroom was in a condemned dry-cleaning business, behind what had been an office complex, now the rest of the school. One afternoon, just before starting, I noticed a van parked at the southern end of my building. There stood a bald man in a red robe, a sash over one shoulder, rope sandals on his feet, talking on a cell phone.

Here? I thought. I waited nearby as he finished his call. I had a question for him.

"Is there any way you could discuss your faith? It is Buddhism, right?"

He smiled kindly and put away his phone. I didn't see where.

"I can do better than that. A mandala is in progress in the building right behind us. You are welcome to come and watch."

I gathered my class and with a gesture of his hand and a turn of his head, he led us to a door, and down a narrow flight of stairs where we stood near the wall to watch the entire floor turn into a masterpiece. As it neared completion, two young monks slipped singular grains of colored sand through their fingers onto the edges of the image. A "Yin/Yang" symbol in the center was surrounded by design elements, all in vibrant colors.

"Do you have questions?" he asked the students.

One boy raised his hand, "What happens to the mandala when it is finished?"

He paused, and in all seriousness said, "It is temporal, made to exist for only a short time."

"So, it will be destroyed?" the boy continued, concerned.

The man gazed thoughtfully at the students, pausing to look at each one, "It represents the transitory nature of life, of this moment even."

He gave them a moment to ponder this. We thanked him and turned to go.

The experience was short lived, miraculous and beautiful. I took them from class without permission slips or even an okay from the office. If I had done all that, most assuredly, we would have missed it, a rare experience, gone, never to be repeated.

At the end of that year the students voted to have a painting class in place of drawing, so I was unhired. However, I would need a recommendation and I approached the principal. He directed me to his secretary to write it as he was occupied, but she was also quite busy also, so he suggested I write it myself. Fine with me. I was given appropriate stationary with the impressive heading, sat at her computer and wrote a clearly supportive letter, stating my qualifications, my ability to relate to high school students and my dedication to their learning.

I don't think he even read it, but he did sign it. I then sought another teaching assignment. This time it turned out to be quite far from town.

66. RURAL LIVES

I was close to giving up my job search in mid-September, two weeks after school had started when, in a small rural town in Arizona, a high school English teacher decided she would rather teach sixth grade. I can't blame her as this is a difficult crowd, but her choice gave me a position.

I was hired to teach 11th grade English and art to the cowboys, farmers, baseball players and their girlfriends. Some of the cowboys were also baseball players, but most had one role. The FFA, Future Farmers of America, was a big deal. In fact, it seemed to be a requirement that students start the year caring for a piglet, protect it through the fall and winter, then sell it in the spring when as the pigs were now full grown. One was to be pit barbecued for the school in a big celebration. The rest were sold somewhere.

I took the teaching position with enthusiasm, but repeatedly heard the mantra from the students, "This is Mayer. Why learn anything?"

It became obvious while observing my class. The back row of students pressed to the wall, had a gum chewer with a cap over his eyes, a red-headed girl in ponytails frantically filling in a coloring book with crayons and one student sitting on a desk behind her boyfriend turned so she could massage his shoulders.

I tried to enthuse them with literature but gave up on the story about tilting windmills. They had no idea what they were so Don Quixote rode off into the sunset. I dedicated a day in February to Frederick Douglas. A week later I learned that one of my students would now be home-schooled as his grandparents, who were raising him, objected to the topic.

Vocabulary turned out to be my greatest success with these students. They liked writing sentences with new words. One girl, inspired by her boyfriend, put him into every sentence, every time. For example, pandemonium: Jimmy saw some pandemonium last night at Circle K. Or reminisce: Jimmy and I reminisce on Friday night. Hardly ever, if at all, could I be sure she grasped the meaning of the words, but she loved writing sentences about Jimmy.

As the snow fell outside, students requested passes to check on their pigs. I looked out to see a whitened world blow past my window and wrote passes as I imagined shivering pink pigs freezing in their pens. I even saw a student in the nurse's office cradling her small piglet in a blanket. True to life.

The baseball players wore the same clothes, white t-shirts and jeans. They chewed tobacco but not in class. Although they understood the dangers of Bull Durham, they had an odd sense of pride, one pulling his cheek to one side to show me missing portions of his mouth. No one smoked cigarettes as far as I could tell.

Occasionally a refugee would arrive from California. I guess the parents thought a small Arizona town would be an ideal place to raise a family. One boy, from Oakland, wore on his first day a bracelet with metal spikes, a chain dangling from his pocket and jeans crumpled around his ankles, his hair in stiff points matching his bracelet.

On my way around the room, I paused at his desk and leaned in, to whisper, "No one dresses like that around here." He pulled back like a bull cornered by a matador, shocked to have a teacher approach him unaffected by his armor. On day two, he dressed like everybody else. I may have saved his life.

Not all the kids here were from Mayer though. Some were bused up the hill from Black Canyon City, several miles south. A girl from there, a slight, tender blond who sat in the front row interrupted class one afternoon, sobbing.

"What's wrong?" I asked, concerned.

She blurted out, "I think I'm pregnant!" Then, "It happened on the school bus."

I had traveled that rough mountain road behind that same bus as it bounced down the hill and tried to visualize the possibility she was talking about.

How? I thought.

But before I could inquire tactfully, she added, "A... fly... flew up my nose!"

The rest of the class sat silently, but from their faces I could tell which ones believed her and those who knew better.

"Uh," I said, "that's not how you get pregnant. You don't have to worry.

Here." I handed her a pass to the nurse. "Talk to her. It will help."

As the year continued, I had my footing, I thought. A detention plan was in place in case anyone had to be sent from class, which did happen sometimes. One day, our truant officer in charge was out sick. Everyone knew there would be no consequences that day. It happened that another student had arrived recently from California. He started a problem with a couple of other boys, so I sent all three out to sit in the hallway, leaving my door open to hear them, giving the rest of the class time to work.

Spit wads started flying out there, but I had my hands full inside with instruction. Except, one of the boys missed his target and a large ball of notebook paper hit me in the head. It didn't hurt, but gasps arose from the students.

I stepped to the door, "I need an apology from someone by the end of the day." I didn't say, "Or else."

Well, school was over, without a confession, and I headed home, wondering what my next step would be to keep my authority.

I didn't need to worry. The next morning, just minutes before the first bell, I heard a sloshing sound from far down the hallway and looked out the door to see Mr. California, dripping wet, leaving puddles where he walked.

I lost the three to detention that day. Our disciplinarian was back.

Excited, one of the Mayer boys ran in to tell me the story.

"We threw him in the horse trough, Ms. Rogers. He did it to the wrong teacher!"

As he started out the door, he turned to add, "Yeah, we have detention, but it was worth it!"

I didn't have to worry about my so-called authority. What they did on my behalf, saved my dignity. I felt like a Rodeo Queen!

67. MY CRIMINALS

I knew I was in for a rough ride during the job interview, but I needed employment, and it paid well.

"You seem like a nice person." The principal's observation. "Are you sure you can do this?"

"Are you saying you don't want nice teachers," I asked, thinking, *"I'm too nice…may be a problem."*

He answered me, "No, no at all, just wondering."

I think I may have been the only applicant, interviewed on Friday, classes starting Monday. I was hired to teach Humanities and Art, given keys with the last words of warning, "One more thing. Don't ever turn your back on them."

This was a county school, set on the grounds of what had been a military base. Classrooms designed for elementary students were now used for much larger bodies. They were the remnants of failure; dropouts, troublemakers and those seeking credit recovery, all mixed together, no designation to figure out who was who. The school had a metal detector at the student gate. This was the year following Columbine.

I went directly to my classroom where I arranged the desks, brought the textbooks out of storage and noticed the door to my storage cabinet was hanging by one hinge.

That first day I had over fifty students in my classroom. I took attendance with the information given, with students situated in desks, on the floor and perched on windowsills.

I explained, "If you all come back there will be another class set up for you."

I believed it. Yet, on day two, fewer than half arrived.

I called their names and one explained that he was to be called Enigma, not Kyle.

However, even his long black flapping trench coat and his metal lunch box holding effigies ready to be cursed, did not influence me. He was Kyle to me. The other students, however, were uneasy. The tension in the air was like static. His flowing black attire alone made a dynamic, threatening statement.

During class one day he took a make-up case from his box and began applying foundation. I reminded him, "Kyle, if you want to put on make-up you have to use the restroom to do so, just like everyone else."

I only heard one short laugh and then silence. Not the normal response from high schoolers.

Another time, he showed me his collection of Dr. Seuss books, stolen from the library, proud of his ability to steal and hopefully read.

Another student, a stocky dark-haired boy, came during lunch one day to share his ink drawings of demons: Satan, skulls, bloody knives, and other scenes of violence in his sketchbook.

What could I do but compliment him on his astonishing talent?

These were perfect, drawn skillfully with detail. Sure, they were violent, but more important than the subject matter was the ability behind the imagery. I believe that if an individual is not accepted as he is, he cannot grow past the stage he is in. Stuck.

Because of my compliments a young man who was brave enough to show me his terrifying art, not knowing how I would react, left beaming with pride. Besides, there is a market for this.

I only had one direct threat that year.

"I will burn you!" the student said coming toward me, something in his hand, hunched down as if about to pounce.

I continued arranging papers on my desk and asked calmly, looking up, "Why would you do that?"

His accusation: "You don't like Jackson Pollack!"

I paused, "Of course, I like Jackson Pollack. I have always liked Jackson Pollack."

I wasn't lying to protect myself. I *do* like his art.

"Okay, then, alright." He retreated, backing up. I think he may have been holding a lighter, but I didn't see it. He turned and left, with me wondering, *"Whatever gave him that idea? And why was Pollack so important to him?"* Still, better not to ask.

Many of them smoked and balanced a cigarette on their ears for convenience I guess. I had noticed an odd white cloud hanging low over a ramada near the classroom. It was square in shape and stayed suspended there every day. Here students and teachers smoked together in its shade, under this white cloud of smoke. When I felt like doing it, I would take a cigarette from one of my student's ears, wiggle it in front of them and hand it back. My way of saying, "Don't smoke." They got the intent and seemed okay with my intrusion on their vice.

On Halloween the young children from preschool on campus, came to "Trick or Treat." These were the children of my students. If I had known I would have bought candy, but a big kid named Sergio was prepared. He sat grinning, a bag of candy between his feet and as each child passed, he dropped candy into their pumpkins. I finally noticed the ankle bracelet. He was happy. The kids were happy, and I didn't need to know his crime.

Still, I had to be watchful. There were times when I would find a note at the bottom of an assignment, informing me of a problem in the class. It helped me be even more observant. Every morning on my way I prayed for radiant acquiescence. Driving home, I often cried.

On Mondays, I rearranged the desks to keep students from forming relationships. The week we studied Egypt, the desks became the edges of a funeral barge. The assignment was to design their own memorial barge using hieroglyphics and art, given a chance to consider their own mortality.

Plato's *The Cave* was the best though. If you are unfamiliar with the setting, imagine being chained to the floor facing a wall. The only thing you see are the shadows passing before you cast there by the firelight behind you. This is your reality.

One prisoner escapes to the real world outside and returns to tell the others that there is more than this, more than this limited life. Yet, unfortunately, in their trapped existence, they find the truth beyond belief.

This was acted out as a drama, students wearing toga sheets, holding flashlights behind the ones seated on the floor, casting shadows on the wall.

Could any one of them see themselves in this parable?

A breakthrough came when I assigned The Memory Project.

"Bring in any object that means something to you, a photo, a souvenir, even a rock you value." It didn't matter what it was. They were to present it to the class sharing the reason it meant something in their lives.

First, picture my class, a mix of Anglo, African American, Mexican, Native American and Asian, none of whom spoke to one another. That was until…One of the first presenters was a black boy holding an 8x10 photo of himself, "This is me when I was in the second grade and lived in Detroit. I really like this picture because of my Afro."

A few others took part, but not all.

Finally, a boy who was known for sticking his foot in the aisle in repeated attempts to trip someone, came up. He pulled a photo from under his arm. "This is me when I was black and lived in Detroit."

Obviously, this white kid had taken the other boy's photo from his desk. I held my breath, uncertain as to how this would go.

He added," Well, if Michael Jackson can do it, so can I."

Laughter broke through the fog of suspicion and filled the room. The tension dissipated and vanished. The students started discussing whether Jackson was still black or now white. They began to talk about race.

The next presenter was Asian, a girl who brought her music. Korean hip-hop made a connection. The room burst into celebration. Everyone wanted to dance. It was a party. They were sharing, becoming a class, becoming friends. It was miraculous even though I think that was the day someone stole my clock. This was my Humanities class.

In another building the art class was crowded, students stuck into small chairs working at low tables in this elementary art room. One assignment was to draw or paint what you want to see outside your window. They did love this assignment.

Another time I asked for an early memory, probably not the best idea. Rosie described being arrested along with her parents when she was still in diapers, her arms raised above her head by order of the police. I gave her oil paints, and everything else she needed. She painted on the canvas, repeatedly, paint on top of paint, never completing it. It was the process that mattered, not the product. Anyone who has held a brush might feel this.

I didn't read the same tension in the art class as in Humanities as they were safely involved in art projects, that is until we made pinatas. We used balloons, covered them with strips of newspaper dipped in wheat paste. The outside would dry, leaving a crisp shell to paint as a pinata, but I didn't consider the consequences of a shrinking balloon. As the withered balloons pulled from the stiff papier mâché, they popped. They popped in sequence, and they popped loudly, sounding like gunfire in close range.

The students carpeted the floor, frozen in fear. I carefully stepped between arms and legs to get one of the pinatas. I cut through the top and pulled out a now limp rubbery mass once a balloon and held it up for all to see. They sighed in unison. They laughed in frayed laughter, and they stood up.

In this class, I also had a student requesting a name change.

"When you take attendance today, Ms. Rogers don't say my name. Call me Two."

"Two?" I asked.

"Yes. Two. I want to be called *Two* from now on."

This was odd since he and his girlfriend walked as one person, her hanging on his shoulder, pressed into his side, keeping in step so they wouldn't fall.

"Okay," I said, but when I took attendance, I said, "Number two?"

He corrected me at once, "No, Ms. Rogers, not Number Two, just Two."

But it was too late. The rest of the class was in hysterics.

"Oh." I said feigning ignorance. "Sorry about that."

At the end of the semester, I found a note on my desk from a girl who had perfect attendance in both my classes, and in fact repeated both classes, yet never did even one assignment. I didn't know why. Something good was happening, I hoped. The note folded in fourths was just left there. I picked it up and opened it.

It read, "I will never, ever forget you." Signed, "Nicole."

I felt honored, like what I was doing mattered.

How had I touched her? I do not know. It isn't always about grades, or achievement. There is more to teaching than that. Here it was, the best tribute I have ever had.

68. JOINING THE CIRCUS

The senior high school yearbook photo tells the world where you plan to go from there. Mine said "English Teacher," but I was a long way from that goal, doing everything else but to avoid meeting up with teenagers. My student teaching experience had left me unprepared for the job in a real high school. I knew literature and grammar, but not how to control a classroom.

It was now or never. Three times I drove around Coronado High School, wondering if I was ready. The job offer was for a 1.5 position in tutoring, which I had been doing, driving through the desert to gated communities where children with busy, wealthy parents needed homework support.

The interview with the principal that morning was delayed by interruptions, urgent school business appearing at her door. When I did enter her office, I noticed a pair of ducks right outside her window, preparing a nest. Of course, I asked.

She explained, "They come here every year, hatch their eggs and leave."

"And no one bothers them?"

"No, the students respect them."

Maybe I was at the right place. If ducks were respected, I would be too.

I was hired and within a couple weeks my part-time tutoring job turned into a full-time teaching position, but one without a classroom, meaning I floated between rooms, evicting the classroom teacher during the prep period. An hour later I moved again.

A solution was available, the bookroom where unused textbooks were stored. If I boxed up shelves of books I could have that room. It was hot in late August, and it was dusty, but I did it, making this classroom my own.

All my students were in a remedial English program, and one petite red-headed girl decided to mouth off every day. However, I had bought that room with my own sweat, and I wasn't going to let her destroy what little confidence I had.

Many years later, while making a bank deposit, there she was. My problem student now a bank teller!

"Do you remember me?" she asked.

"Of course, I do," I replied with kindness in my voice.

"I'm married now, and I have a little boy."

"Wonderful!" I say with genuine happiness for her.

Then, after a second or two of uncomfortable silence, she asked, "Was I a bad student?"

What can I say? "You were a mess," or "No," or "Never."

"You just needed time to grow up and here you are." Smiling, I said, "It is very good to see you again, doing so well." I meant it.

That's what I like about teaching teenagers. There's always hope.

In September of that year, I walked past another English teacher's classroom and noticed the transparency she had projected on the screen as a writing prompt. It was an image of a tilted high rise, windows half open, people falling, above a city where an airplane was flying close, too close for comfort. It didn't mean a thing to me until I walked by the same room the next morning where the TV showed smoke pouring from a New York structure engulfed in flames, shortly after, a plane ramming into another building.

How can art precede life? What would make that teacher choose that image? What did the students write the day before? On that day we all watched the reality in silence and horror.

One mantra that held me up was the conviction that something would go wrong every day: The copy machine was broken. My key broke off in the door lock. The elevator would go down but not up. The fire drill interrupted my timed writing assignment, and on and on.

The second calming thought that kept me secure was the understanding that high school was a circus with a rat race going on at the same time. Three minutes allowed students to go across campus, to go to the restroom, get books from their lockers, travel through opposing lemmings to navigate to the next class and be seated before the bell rang. Teachers had to stand in line to make copies, use the restroom, check e-mail and return a call from the principal. That was the rat race. The circus went on all the time.

69. PLAY THEIR GAMES

Looking at any group of teenagers, one might consider them to be mature because they look that way. Physically they are complete, some even looking older than their years. This is deceiving. They are not ready to contribute in the way we expect. We overestimate them because they look so grown up. If you doubt it, read the book, *Primal Teen*, a brain based analysis of the years from twelve to the early twenties using scans on real children to record brain development. Synapses connect, yet not enough to furnish what is required, not for several years. They still need direction and guidance as this happens all the time inside their heads. They want discipline, but they act like they don't. We all know this.

I learned early on to respond to their games with my own. One kid who wanted my attention looked at me, eyes lowered, snapped his fingers and motioned for me to come to him. I was shocked, but I didn't show it. I returned his gestures in the same way. I lowered my eyes, looked at him, snapped my fingers and beckoned for him to come to me, and he did. That ended it. He never gave me any trouble after that.

Literature is more than reading stories. American lit disturbed me, but my first year I had juniors, so I had no choice. First there are the suffering Pilgrims, followed by a sermon, "Sinners in the Hands of an Angry God." Of course, there's Nathaniel Hawthorne and "The Crucible," witch burning. Finally, one of my favorites, Emerson, came along. In his honor I assigned my students a nighttime experience. *Lie on the grass, look up at the sky, follow the clouds across the moon, feel the breeze, smell the air and write about it.* Few, if any, had ever done this before. They liked this assignment. and I hoped they would do it again on their own.

I just couldn't get excited about much of the curriculum, but by February we had Frederick Douglas, Martin Luther King, Jr., Jackie Robinson and Malcolm X, whose story about getting a conk generated all kinds of essays on personal hair problems, lots of chewing gum in hair and haircuts done by themselves. At last, we were on a contemporary issue.

Finally, I landed on world literature, sophomores, fourteen-year-olds, and I happily moved into this subject. It was open and expanding all the time.

A speech by Vaclav Havel, former president of Poland, shared current examples of cultural mixes, for example: a Bedouin nomad on a camel drinking a coke. Havel made us recognize our connections and differences. He described the miraculous creation of our planet, Gaia, explaining how slender the chance was for our world to even exist, ending with the conviction that our survival depends on the recognition of our shared humanity. That semester one of my students had her head shaved to donate money to a cause she believed in.

There was a time that all the students were required to write a business letter in *every single class,* including algebra and P. E. I could not do this and bore my classes. My students would write to an alien in a business-like format. They might write a formal letter of complaint about the mess the aliens left behind in the cornfield, for example, or a query letter about jobs on their planet, or even a request to join them as an intern. It fulfilled the requirement, my way.

Sometimes serious learning could turn humorous as was the case during sixth hour one afternoon. We were reading the play by George Bernard Shaw about *Joan of Arc,* my all-time favorite heroine. At the dramatic point when she hears her voices, at that very moment, my phone, set on low, played my ring tone by Leonard Cohen. My friend, Eleanor, was changing clothes in a dressing room at her doctor's office when she bumped her phone, and it called me.

My students heard the soft voices of what they imagined were angels floating invisibly above them singing "Hallelujah… Hallelujah… Halle…lu…oo…jah."

Struggling to keep from laughing, I held up my ringing phone to show them, For a few seconds they were true believers. But the fact that it was timed so perfectly shows that someone has a sense of humor, maybe God or Joan or both.

However, after thirteen years of this joyous experience, a bogus threat from the superintendent made me decide to retire early. We were told that 1% of our pay would be required for administrative expenses. I was already tutoring after school on Wednesdays, teaching an English as Second Language class Monday nights for parents, this, plus a remedial reading summer class would be my 1%. Time to go.

After I completed the paperwork for my retirement, I felt much more relaxed. So relaxed, I was easy to lie to my students, at least one morning.

It was second hour, between nine and ten o'clock, when a boy stumbled in close to twenty minutes late. I suspected drugs. I told him I would send him to the nurse because he seemed ill.

While I was calling security, not the nurse, he attempted to pass a bottle of Jack Daniels to a sweet girl whose mother was in my ESL night class. Soon he was escorted out.

Without a close examination, I thought the spot on the floor near his desk looked suspicious. I took out my yellow caution tape which I had saved for such an occasion as this and cordoned off the desks so no one in the next class would be revolted. Then I call the janitor, Mark, who arrived with a vacuum, rags, a mop and bucket, all possible tools to attack what would have been disgusting had it been true. He recognized it for what it was, chewing gum. He sighed and left.

He seems so disappointed," one student remarked.

The next class arrived just after I shoved the pile of tape into the trash can. One kid, Kyle, came in as I was taking attendance, late as usual. He noticed the enticing bright yellow tape, pulled it out and wrapped it around himself. He had been annoying all year and now it was May. My last chance.

"I wouldn't do that if I were you," I said in a serious, warning tone.

"Somebody vomited in that waste can."

He couldn't strip the tape off his body fast enough!

"You better go to the restroom and clean up, be sure to wash your hands really well!"

As soon as the door shut, I faced my class, smiling.

"I lied. Nobody threw up in the waste basket."

Their laughter, half in relief and half for the justice of it, told me how much they had enjoyed seeing this kid suffer.

It also showed how tired they were of his stuff because, when he came back in, no one said anything. They just sat there grinning.

70. WAR TORN

The Garfield cat poster on the door to my classroom read "Start Thinking Now!" I should've chosen the one that said, "You are not immune to propaganda."

I wanted my students to know how to recognize truth but teaching the difference between fact and opinion proved to be challenging. It seems our culture, often news programs, blur these lines.

As they began writing persuasively, the students needed to provide support: facts, examples, quotes, etc. To clarify the difference in a dramatic manner, I rented the video," Outfoxed," a visual representation of how this news outlet manipulates information, without providing the sources.

A newscaster standing on a pristine, sparkling clean beach declared that the oil spill by BP was clearly not a problem. Where was this beach? No one knows! Repeatedly, throughout the video, various people spoke this phrase, "Some people say…" in front of some unverified statement.

My point in showing this was only to expose flaws, when no factual support was included, to simply prepare my students to be accurate in their own writing.

However, one parent was angered by this. I do not know what provoked her, maybe she worked for the network? I will never know, but she complained vigorously to the district superintendent, and I was called in to the principal's office to explain myself, which I did.

I thought it ended there.

Yet, I still had more to teach, Visual Persuasion, the kind that sneaks up on you in advertising and political ads. People are either shown in their best attire or doomed to be seen in droopy sweatpants pushing a lawn mower.

Following the invasion of Iraq thousands of smiling citizens were shown waving small American flags, seemingly in gratitude for the overthrow of Saddam Hussein.

"Where do you think these people got these flags?" I asked my students.

Nothing. No response.

I support our government. I believe in our country. I only wanted my students to think, just to think about what they were seeing.

Finally, I had to ask other questions.

"Do you think they had these flags in their pockets? Or do you think they were handed out for a photo opportunity?

This got me in trouble again, in the principal's office, accused.

"This was political!"

"I didn't intend it to be," I responded with seriousness, believing in the value of knowing the truth, no matter what.

"I only want my students to be those who look at the world and factor out what they see with what they are told."

Nothing happened, and I went back to the same exact teaching method with the novel *The Things They Carried* by Tim O'Brien.

The books were stored on shelves, never used, brand new, just waiting for me to grab them. I passed them out, documenting the student's name with the number on the assigned text.

"What did these Marines carry?"

As we read, we learned it wasn't the forty plus pounds of weaponry, food, water, and clean socks they struggled with. It was the weight of war.

The dialogue of soldiers at war includes words I never would allow in my classroom, for example the F word. In the novel, a landmine sends an unsuspecting trooper skyward into a tree, in pieces. The word used reflects the honest reaction of a man whose buddy in gone in an instant.

The principal asked for a copy one Friday afternoon, but on Monday when I needed the book back, I sent a student after it.

"Ms. Rogers, all the F words are highlighted in yellow!"

I wondered, "Did he read the book or just look for ammunition to use against me?"

I knew it would not be long before I would be called in again, but I had my own ammo after I explained the issue to the school librarian. There it was the title, *The Things They Carried* by Tim O'Brien, near the top of the published list of recommended reading for college-bound students. After this, the harassment ended. I had won a small war of my own.

Then they sent in the Marines, or rather one Marine with an invitation for my class to visit the Career Center to listen to what he had offer. One handsome, impressive Marine dressed in a uniform, decorated with red braid, a gold emblem on his sleeve, a white hat on his head was offering trinkets, key chains and stickers, to my students. They sat across from the table where he stood, magnificent in his dress blues, his offerings displayed before them.

While he presented his opportunities, my students looked down or around, but not one of them looked at him directly. As we left, they passed by the souvenirs offered without even a glance, and every week following, as the year progressed, one of the boys in that class gave a body count of the American soldiers at least once a week.

"Ms. Rogers, twenty-two died yesterday."

All of us paused for a moment of silence.

"Thank you for letting us know." Near tears, I kept going.

They were no less American than that beautiful Marine. They just weren't buying the noise.

– Chapter 9 –

71. THE CHAIR

If you swing a necklace slowly in front of someone and say the magic words you can hypnotize that person. At least, that's what I thought. My sister wouldn't succumb to my scheme even though I repeated the words, "You are getting sleepy… sleepee… sleeepee."

She wouldn't even pretend and no one else would let me try, so I gave up.

What were those magic words?

As an adult, seeking closure on childhood issues.

Did those things really happen?

I asked to be hypnotized during counseling, to pay attention to the technique, especially the words. I was told to relax, I remember, and then he said something which I do not recall.

Just like that, I was six years old again, sitting at my place at the table, on my chair, writing my name for the first time. I was aware I was hypnotized, feeling my current self in the background watching, but the child, me, was real too.

I was in that body, holding that pencil tightly, drawing the tall line on the left side of the letter A. The sound of my mother in the kitchen nearby, the dim light from the lamp hanging above the table, the reflection of it on the window against the night sky, and the wicker seat of my familiar chair comforted me. This chair, with the cane seat, had a ladder back and rungs on which I was not supposed to set my restless feet, already scarred by the scuffing I did back and forth with my shoes.

The letter A had only one side done when I reappeared in front of the counselor. I was highly disappointed in this as I felt so happy being six writing my name. The session ended, having learned nothing about my childhood traumas.

Years later, I stopped at a used furniture store. It was the place where I had sold my mother's table and chairs, including the one I sat in under hypnosis. However, it had been eight or more years, and I had completely forgotten about that.

What I was looking for didn't matter. I was just checking out the place for possibilities.

The sound of water plopping into a bucket led me toward the back of the shop where a hole in the ceiling let in rainwater from the night before, steadily dropped into a pail.

Right next to it, I found a chair, a ladder back, cane seat, complete with scuff marks on the rung where a child's unruly feet moved back and forth while writing the letter A.

The chair and I recognized one another, and my heart went forward to meet an old friend.

I paid eighteen dollars for the memory. It went home with me, a rescued piece of my childhood. I couldn't sit in it, as the seat was torn, and it wasn't beautiful anymore, but it was priceless to me, worth more than the eighteen dollars I spent to give it the respect it deserved.

A couple years passed. It was beyond repair.

I took it to the alley and stood at attention.

I saluted the chair that gave me security, one place that was mine during the long years I was becoming myself.

72. I DECLARE

I got bashed in the head every Sunday in the church nursery. Only a toddler, I recall the exact moment a child with a large head would toddle over to me wobbling, her head floating left and right like a toy top losing its spin. I could not move fast enough, so whatever she had in her hand came crashing down on me.

I didn't want to go there anymore, suffering this weekly, at age two. My mother tried to supplicate on her behalf, "That little girl has something called water on the brain. She won't live very long." I guess I was supposed to feel compassion, but I felt relief, knowing her end would be soon, just not soon enough for me.

Sitting in the wooden pew next to my mother was safer, but uncomfortable and boring. As I got older I was allowed to scribble along the borders of the church bulletin while looking at the backs of people's heads. A red fox with beady eyes peered back at me. Draped around a woman's neck it kept its stare. I was hypnotized, deciding never, ever to wear a dead animal around my own neck.

By the time I was six, I had heard lots of stories, lions ready to pounce on Daniel, a woman's baby about to be sliced in two and Adam and Eve leaving the garden, due to only taking a bite of an apple. All very violent. Questions followed.

Why this and why that and then what? At a church potluck, one question arose in my mind.

"Go ask the preacher," my mother advised.

I found him hungrily eating mashed potatoes and gravy, his mouth full. So, I waited politely next to him.

"Excuse me, I have a question." He stopped eating.

"If Cain killed Abel and he had to leave, where did all the people come from? Who did Cain marry?"

He barely turned his head, and said, "I don't know."

He continued eating his meal not once considering the gravity of a question asked by a child.

If he doesn't know, who does?

I began at that moment to question the entire operation.

I might have been known as "a seeker," never ready to just accept what I was told. Yet, I was a true believer, refusing to give up due to the abundance of beauty I saw in the world. His creation nurtured me.

Still, one question nagged me that I never bothered asking since my first experience with theological authority had failed.

My question was, Why if there is only one God, are there so many religions?

Finally, after many years, I got my answer.

As an artist I had postcards printed of one of my etchings, *Universal Child*, in which the outline of a sparkling child looks heavenward while other figures mill around the fair immersed in the games and rides. My intention was to depict the spiritual world within our material world. I gave this postcard to an artist when I delivered an edition of her prints. She looked carefully at it, and remarked, "You might be a Baha'i and not know it."

"What's that?" I asked.

I learned that there was not a simple answer, but she told me there were nine prophets, including two new ones.

I was intrigued. Now, I could ask my question.

"All religion is connected," she told me.

I understood it as sequential.

She continued, "Revelations or prophets have appeared approximately every thousand years, for example, Abraham, Moses, Zoroaster and others, such as Buddha. The problem is the refusal of the established faith to recognize the new one, making countless choices available, confusing the issue, causing wars over religion."

A few weeks went by, and I read as much as I could find. I learned there would be a Fireside, a social gathering inviting questions, to be held on a Friday night, but when my friend called to get the address, the person didn't speak English.

"Call back," I said.

This might be my only chance to meet these people.

A second call gave us an English speaker and we went.

That night, after hearing the story of the origin of this Faith, I announced without hesitation," I want to declare." (A confession of faith as the Christians call it.)

Now, at last, women were valued, prejudice would end, and world peace was promised. The room erupted in celebration. I was more than accepted; I was embraced. I had no idea of the rarity of what I had done. They don't advertise. They don't proselytize. You must find one to become one.

A dream that I had months before now made sense. Way back when my grandmother was living, she had a picture of Christ on her living room wall. On a road high above Jerusalem, He sits pondering the view of the temple, its dome gleaming gold. The scene was nearly identical in my dream. The road was the same, as was the sky, but there was a difference. The temple may have been there, but a door blocked the view. Framed in bricks, this door stood alone, unattached to a building, just this door.

In my dream, I opened it and went in. It was completely dark. I traced my hands along the walls on both sides as I went farther into the passageway, but as I walked, the walls gradually narrowed until I was wedged in, no longer able to move, stuck, trapped by these walls in total darkness. I never cried. I just didn't, but this time I did. I sobbed, alone, without hope and in despair.

Then, suddenly, I was outside again, facing the front of the door I had just entered. I sensed someone near me and turned to see an older gentleman behind me. He had white hair and a beard and was wearing a turban and a cloth robe.

"You have gone as far as you can on your own," he said. "I will help you from now on."

I didn't know it then, but in that dream, I met Abdul Baha, the son of the new prophet. Comforted, my fears disappeared. my question finally answered.

73. FIFTY PLUS FOUR

Before I knew about a calendar or even a clock, I set up a time to meet. I would meet myself still waiting at age four to tell myself the truth when I was fifty-four. The child I had saved was me, and I had forgotten to mark down the appointment. It found me anyway, unprepared, terrifying, just as it had been on that long ago morning when I stood in front of the camera saying, "Take my picture! Get closer!"

Who was I now?

Certainly not the trembling child, but she jumped into me, and I remembered.

I fought at that moment to stay conscious, to keep myself from disappearing into some vast, spaceless, mindless universe from which I could not return.

The morning classes for summer camp had ended.

I was free to fall apart as parents picked up their children.

In the bathroom I held on, to stay within myself. I had to concentrate, to focus, on the floor, the wall, the sidewalk, the physical things I could see and count on.

Hold on, I told myself. Stay aware.

Fighting the loss of consciousness while walking, I made my way to the door of the office of the person in charge of the safety of children, not a priest, a counselor who gave the rules on day one, for the prevention of sexual abuse. At the time this was the first possible admission by the Catholic church on the issue of priests and children. He was someone who would understand.

If you have ever felt the feeling of losing your mind, you are lucky to have saved it.

I am sure some of us have reached that point of stress and terror. The blank stare on the face of a soldier who has seen too much, or children orphaned by war aimlessly wandering empty streets were me. I was one of them. Now I had to face the past. I knocked on his office door and was invited in, thankful to be in a safe place and to sit where I could hold on, to feel somewhat stable.

He was so kind, and I was so needy.

I told him my story from the beginning, explaining how I thought a bear had been eating me. I knew differently now, but the child did not know. I told him how I insisted on that photo, and the way I protected my child mind by sending a message into now.

Here I had the consequences, yet grateful to the young me who knew exactly what to do, to send this possible plunge into oblivion to the only person who could save me, my own adult self.

As I talked, he listened. His familiarity with stories like mine gave me a sense of peace. I wasn't the only adult who had recovered lost memories. He knew many more. He arranged his time to meet with me at the end of every day as the camp continued.

He explained that our bodies hold experience on a cellular level, beyond our mind's ability to remember, our skin remembers.

I was mending, cell by cell.

A touch on your shoulder, or a pull on your arm can trigger an emotional response and a full-blown visual can return. I believe he spoke from his own trials, knowing the full cost of childhood sexual abuse.

But I had work to do. David, I will call him, gave me a book, *Courage to Heal*, a thick paperback full of exercises designed to work through the mess of a troubled childhood. I followed through the entire thing.

At the same time, I had to find a place to live. My roommate had vacated. I could no longer afford to stay. In the teacher's workroom, in the middle of my new crisis, I reluctantly shared the bad news with my colleagues. Without hesitation, the head of our English department, the kindest woman on the face of this Earth offered me a place to stay, a spare room in her home, one she made available from time to time for refugees like me. It was unbelievable and I accepted at once and gratefully.

For David, who entered my life at the very instant I needed him, I did a painting, 11" x 14", oil on canvas, gray clouds parting with sunlight breaking through. It took every bit of my inner resolve to supply the strength to finish it and paint the sides of the support. I felt incredibly weak. Depression had enveloped me at the end of this emotional ride. I felt I was a failure with nothing to show for my existence.

"I have nothing, nothing of my own, just my dog, Shay. I have no home!"

I considered my life to be a tragedy.

I told him so, but he said firmly, "No! Your life is a triumph over tragedy!"

"Take your dog. Find a tree. Sit under it every day. Make it your tree, your home for now."

So, I did.

I took Shay to the park, took her to the most appealing tree, although slender, and while I sat under this scrawny, newly planted Arizona tree, I remembered another tree.

One morning during the summer I was four, in Indianapolis, where I freely wandered the neighborhood, and this story started, I found a place surrounded by an aging white picket fence. A metal sign with raised letters leaned awkwardly at the open entrance. I went in.

The tree I met there was no ordinary tree. Its branches spread, reaching the edges of the lot. The trunk was so huge I could not see past it. I walked around this immense tree over and over again, around and around I went, tracing my hand along its ancient bark.

Years later, I learned about the Kile Oak, this very tree planted sometime around the arrival of the Pilgrims, a sturdy, established, eternal tree. This would be my tree, protecting me, keeping me safe. I didn't need to be under it or even near it. I felt it as a memory, there whenever I needed it, replacing the worst of my life with the best I could hope for, getting back strength, independence and mostly faith in myself. Forever thankful to the child I once was who saved me.

EPILOGUE

I was sleeping when the call came. I reached for the phone next to the bed, "Hello?" Wondering who would be calling in the middle of the night?

She answered, "It's me."

Then I understood it was just a dream, my mother had died recently, and this was not real.

I was surprised to hear from her, and asked as always, "How are you?"

"I don't think I am ready for this."

Did she mean she wasn't prepared for heaven?

"If anyone is ready, you are," I said, encouraging her as much as I could.

Good God! I found at least six Bibles at her home after she was gone.

"Mom, you are going to be fine."

"Well," she sighed, thanks for the vote of confidence. I have to go. This is long distance."

That was it, my last communication with my mother.

Days after the dream I found this verse, "You shall find me in the heaven of my Lord, immersed in an ocean of light."

I also learned the true meaning of her name, Lucile, (which she always spelled with only one L.) Light. Her name meant light.

It makes perfect sense as she was a mentor, an example of personal power. She made me find my own light, never interfering in life lessons, giving me room to struggle and work my own way in or out of situations. Neglect, maybe, but I survived, and I was free, with wrong turns and short cuts along the way, imperfect but still here and grateful to have been the child of such a woman.

If you enjoyed this book,
please consider jotting a review about it on the
Andrea Rogers book page at Amazon.com.

DISCUSSION QUESTIONS FOR BOOK CLUBS

1. Discuss the impact the early childhood trauma. How does it change relationships? The author's self-image? Her opinion of life?
2. Has the author made the events real to the reader? Is the writing honest? Do you find humor in the stories, and do they capture your attention?
3. Are the events unusual or common to childhood? Did you as a reader have any similar things happen in your life?
4. Was your way of thinking and questioning the world like the author's, for example, understanding death, feminism, race?
5. Discuss the way the author relates to her mother?? In what way does her mother use stories and poetry? Why? What is her parenting style?
6. Spiritual influences are part of this story. Do these events happen to others or are they unique to the author?
7. How do topics such as racism, religion, women's rights and family history form the author's views?
8. How has her character evolved into adulthood based on the way she lived her childhood?

9. Is the reappearance of the event in the fifty-four-year-old photograph resolved for the reader? What emotions if any affect you at this point in the book?
10. Is the conclusion satisfactory? Is the mother forgiven?

ACKNOWLEDGMENTS

Tempe Public Library's Writer's Forum helped this book become a reality. Until 2019, the story was swimming in my head, but I entered *Thanksgiving* in the competition and won that year's prize in the memoir category. I began to believe my words had purpose, so I joined The Writer's Connection. This gave me a secure consistent opportunity to share, obtain feedback, and gain the encouragement to continue. For these two programs, I need to thank Jill Brenner who created and supported the efforts of writers like me through these opportunities and others, such as Writers in Residence.

I also want to acknowledge all the individual writers in the "Connection" who listened and gave their valued opinions.

For the friends who were roped into listening to my stories, thanks for your patience.

To my daughter, I know my persistence can be annoying. Just forgive me, as I needed your input.

My first editor, Sharon Skinner, kindly gave me hope. Ann Videan, my Book Shepherd, made it final. Both came to me also due to Jill Brenner's dedication to authorship.

A special thanks to my cover designer Russ Anderson.

ABOUT THE AUTHOR

Andrea Rogers began her writing career as a seven-year-old with a travelogue documenting the trip from Indianapolis, Indiana, to Phoenix, Arizona, to visit her grandmother over Christmas break. She knew enough to start the first word with a capital letter and put a period at the end. Her love of language started there.

Northern Arizona University provided a Bachelor of Science in Education with a minor in art. These two subjects fought for dominance most of her life. The two strands of DNA complemented each other as Andrea worked as an artist, with visuals depicting relevant ideas as challenging concepts to be examined.

Facebook: http://www.facebook.com/andrearogersart
Email: akrogersart@gmail.com

www.ingramcontent.com/pod-product-compliance
Lightning Source LLC
Chambersburg PA
CBHW050327010526
44119CB00050B/705